They took their fights into the streets in marches, rallies, political meetings and strikes. And some of their enemies responded not only in print but with abuse, threats and even bomb-throwing.)

They struggled to forge a community with the proletariat; they harassed the governments of the Right and pushed the Left into political and social action. Most importantly, they struggled also to force France to quit the murderous and destructive colonial wars in Indochina and Algeria. There is a parallel with the United States in 1968, carrying on a war in Vietnam that many American intellectuals and writers think equally disastrous as France's Algerian war.

This is also an account of the bitter public rows among these men, and between them and the then-monolithic, Stalinist Communist line—particularly the profound quarrel that was set off when the Russians put down the Hungarian Revolution.

The most famous and most bitter quarrel occurred between the two most glamorous of the Left intellectuals, Sartre and Camus. In an additional chapter, Bernard Murchland narrates this famous, but not always well-understood, dispute that caused a scandal. Mr. Murchland states that theirs was a quarrel between two opposing, incompatible views of man—a struggle in which "everyone who is concerned with the course of history will be a participant...."

Choice of
Action

Choice of Action

The French Existentialists on the Political Front Line

BY MICHEL-ANTOINE BURNIER

TRANSLATED BY BERNARD MURCHLAND

WITH AN ADDITIONAL CHAPTER

BY BERNARD MURCHLAND:

Sartre and Camus—The Anatomy of a Quarrel

Random House *New York*

It is not a matter of choosing one's age
but of choosing one's self within it.

—Jean-Paul Sartre, *What Is Literature?*

List of Abbreviations Used

S.F.I.O. Section Française de l'Internationale Ouvrière
C.G.T.U. Confédération Générale du Travail Unitaire
R.D.R. Rassemblement Démocratique Révolutionnaire
M.R.P. Mouvement Républicain Populaire
C.N.R. Conseil National de la Résistance
R.P.F. Rassemblement du Peuple Français
P.C.I. Parti Communiste International
C.G.T.-F.O. Confédération Générale du Travail Force Ouvrière
U.D.S.R. Union Démocratique et Socialiste de la Résistance
C.A.D. Comité d'Action Démocratique
U.F.D. Union des Forces Démocratiques
P.S.A. Parti Socialiste Autonome
U.G.S. Union de la Gauche Socialiste
F.L.N. Front de Libération Nationale
U.N.E.F. Union Nationale des Etudiants de France
G.P.R.A. Gouvernement Provisoire de la République à Alger
C.F.T.C. Confédération Française des Travailleurs Chrétiens

Preface

MANY PEOPLE have at one time or another in their lives claimed to be "existentialists." Many more have, rightly or wrongly, been associated with this current of thought by critics who like easy labels.

In this book I shall discuss men whose system of thought is "atheistic" existentialism in the strict sense of the word. It is, of course, legitimate to speak of existentialist tendencies in contemporary Christian philosophy. But there is little in common between the devout Gabriel Marcel, who writes prefaces to pamphlets for Moral Rearmament and signed a petition for French Algeria, and Jean-Paul Sartre.

Thus we shall deal with men whose philosophy found its first basic formulation in *Being and Nothingness* and *The Phenomenology of Perception.*[1]

In 1945 they founded *Les Temps Modernes*. With a "common spirit," they wanted "in the long run to clarify a general policy" on the political and social problems of our time. Philosophers like Jean Wahl and Jean Hyppolite did not share this spirit and consequently fall outside the scope of this study.

Our criterion is therefore twofold: philosophical kinship and collaboration on *Les Temps Modernes*. Our basic

1 · Sartre, J.-P., *Being and Nothingness: An Essay on Phenomenological Ontology*, tr. Hazel Barnes (London, Methuen, 1957). Merleau-Ponty, M., *Phenomenology of Perception*, tr. Colin Smith (London, Routledge & Kegan, 1962).

reference is the journal itself. The articles that appeared there are (or were) representative of the existentialists' commitments and positions. When Sartre and Merleau-Ponty separated there were two divergent tendencies of thought until 1956, when dialogue was renewed.

M.-A. B.

Contents

Contents

Choice of
Action

Introduction

Les Temps Modernes did not suddenly appear on the scene, fully armed for political combat, the common cause of a certain group of intellectuals. Its gestation was slow and only gradually did it lay its foundations and define its orientation. It would be a mistake to judge the relationships between a Sartre or a Merleau-Ponty and political life only after they became publicly known. For it was in terms of their reaction against errors of the prewar period as well as their own errors that Sartre and Merleau-Ponty founded the journal and committed themselves to political action. In 1938–39 they realized that they were letting their lives be robbed from them.

In the beginning those who were to become "the existentialists" were "a-political, against all forms of engagement, although with Leftist sympathies like everyone else." [1] They were glad the established order existed so they "could drop their word-bombs on it." Sartre described this state of mind in *The Paths of Freedom*. His protagonist, Mathieu Delarue, a professor of philosophy, detested capitalism and rebelled against it. But he did not really want it suppressed because then he would have had nothing to rebel against, and he relished rebellion immensely. Mathieu is not Sartre; or rather he is a Sartre who would not write and therefore was deprived of any reason for living. Nonetheless, he expresses well the attitude of the writer confronted by the pre-1939 political situation: a spontaneous sympathy for the proletariat, a distant admiration for the Russian Revolution, a certain attraction for the Communist Party, but totally inactive and freed for no reason, with lots of abstract ideas but at bottom disinterested. Such hostility for the bourgeoisie "remained individualistic, *ergo* bourgeois: It was not so very different from that which Flaubert attributed to the 'grocers' and Barrès to the 'barbarians,'" as Simone de Beauvoir remarked in *The Prime of Life*.[2] She confessed that she and Sartre were afraid of losing all freedom in an eventual socialist regime. Even in opposition they took the capitalist system for granted and by no means sought to overthrow it.

The notion of collective *praxis** was absent from their philosophy. Their conception of man, although it violently repudiated spiritualism and introspection, was nonetheless highly idealistic. It rejected the essentialism of souls (slaves, Germans, Jews . . .), of the eternal feminine and all the inscriptions written in a rational heaven. But it did not go beyond a universalist individualism which was not fundamentally different from Descartes. Liberty has two aspects: "On the one hand it is the very modality of life which in one way or another leaves its imprint on all external events; on the other, the concrete possibilities of freedom vary with different individuals," Simone de Beauvoir pointed out. This was the old Stoic distinction between freedom and power that Descartes had used.

The introduction of the idea of power was an attempt to base human action in materialism. Nonetheless—and this is apparent in the first essays of Simone de Beauvoir—man forges, in an almost extra-mundane way, a solitary project.

---

* The Greek word *praxis* is roughly equivalent to deed or action. In Sartre's usage it refers to man's purposeful activity.—B.M.

To be sure his project must be realized in this world, among men. But man's investiture by the collectivity and his situation were not described. The Other then seemed to be an accident and the world a simple condition; in this framework, it was up to each individual to work out his salvation with whatever means he had at hand.

Thus we can understand why Jean-Paul Sartre, Simone de Beauvoir and Maurice Merleau-Ponty were not concerned with History. They had to justify their existence; for this it was enough, as Sartre claimed, that they "write and create beautiful books." The proletariat's struggle was a good thing for the proletariat but not of concern to the intellectuals. Sartre liked to repeat at that time that membership in the Communist Party was the only way of salvation for the proletariat, but that other roads were available for the writer. To each his own.

Colette Audry opposed this view. Impregnated with Marx and Trotsky, a member of the Education Federation of the C.G.T.U. since 1932 and the S.F.I.O. during the leadership of Marceau-Pivert since 1935, she considered herself a militant engaged in a struggle. She could not remain neutral before the situation. "You see the world like a post office," she told Sartre, who answered that "the world *is* a post office."

Did he have any inkling that among the employees some had privileged positions as stamp collectors while others did the work?

Sartre never voted (even for the election of the Popular Front) and only reluctantly accepted a union card. He and Simone de Beauvoir sometimes attended demonstrations of the united Left after 1934, but it never occurred to them "to parade, sing or shout with the others." "This more or less represented our attitudes at the time," said Simone de Beauvoir. "Events could arouse strong emotions in us, whether anger, fear, or joy, but we did not participate in them. We remained spectators." [3]

Sartre scorned the political pretensions of intellectuals. While listening to the results of the 1936 elections, he heard Chamson shout triumphantly: "What a beating we're giving them!" "Chamson never gave any sort of beating to anyone," Sartre remarked impatiently. "Talk, declamations, manifestoes, propaganda—what a lot of pointless fuss!" Nonetheless Sartre and Simone de Beauvoir gave everything they could to collections that were taken up for strikers.

The "philosophy of contingency" was too greedy for reality—and left too many doors open—not to eventually undergo a radical mutation that would put it in contact with the world of men. In its abstract phase it risked losing itself in being an ideology that simply described the uprootedness and solitude of a certain number of intellectuals. While it seemed to cut off all contact with the bourgeoisie, it had no ties with the proletariat and floated empty and absent. But, however ignorant it was of society, it nevertheless gained from its many crises. For a long time Sartre's thought had been groping toward "the *reality* of Marxism, the heavy presence on my horizon of the masses of workers, an enormous somber body which *lived* Marxism, which *practiced* it and which at a distance exercised an irresistible attraction on *petit-bourgeois* intellectuals. . . . But when it [Marxist philosophy] was presented as a real determination of the proletariat and as the profound meaning of its acts—for itself and in itself—then Marxism attracted us irresistibly without our knowing it, and it put all our acquired culture out of shape." [4]

Thus forging a certain number of theoretical concepts that later would be the basis for political practice, Sartre from 1934 on called historical materialism "a prolific working hypothesis" and was thinking of "laying the philosophical basis for absolutely positive moral and political attitudes." [5] He was also aware of the necessity, as described by Hegel, of the I for the existence of the Other. The generosity of Sartre and de Beauvoir saved them even in their individualism from becoming mere intellectual adventurers. They could not accept the "intoxication of intensity or power" of a Malraux, of which Mounier sometimes accused them. But their philosophy needed an incarnation —almost a destruction—in order to *realize* itself. It was not in itself capable of irrupting into History. It was necessary for History, hidden and distant for those who were not consciously making it, to irrupt suddenly into life. The weight of tradition and the bourgeoisie was too strong to be transformed by Colette Audry's criticism or the example of the Communist Paul Nizan. It took the war to make the future existentialists see reality. In retreat they felt compromised and responsible for what they had not done. Munich was a brutal awakening. "Then, suddenly, History burst over me, and I dissolved into fragments. I woke to find myself scattered over the four quarters of the globe, linked by every nerve in me to each and every other individual. All my ideas and values were turned upside down," Simone de Beauvoir wrote in *The Prime of Life*.

The Roads of Freedom was an account of this entrance into the front lines of History. Until then Sartre's fictional characters—Roquentin, Lucien Fleurier, and so forth— lived individual lives. After Munich they were caught up in collective history. "At once actors and witnesses, executioners and victims, they no longer knew where their responsibilities began or ended," Colette Audry wrote. Sartre described this discovery in *The Reprieve*: "One hundred million free consciousnesses, each aware of the walls, the glowing stump of a cigar, familiar faces, and each constructing its destiny on its own responsibility. And yet each of those consciousnesses, by imperceptible contacts and insensible changes, realizes its existence as a cell in a gigantic and invisible coral: everyone is free, and yet the stakes are set. It is there, it is everywhere, it is the totality of all my thoughts, of all Hitler's words, of all Gomez's acts: but no one is there to make that total. It exists solely for God. But God does not exist. And yet the war exists." [6]

Mathieu Delarue then understood his failure. Freedom is not an end in itself, not a flower to preserve. He realized that he was part of a human life in which no man could be truly uncommitted. The first cause of the war was men's discouragement and cowardice. War was inevitable after Munich—Sartre and Merleau-Ponty were convinced of this. This meant that their inactivity during the prewar period was not a retreat from an absolutely indifferent world but resignation—permissiveness toward History and those who were leading it toward catastrophe. Given this, the question then became: What attitude should men adopt in the future? Sartre, Simone de Beauvoir and Merleau-Ponty responded that things could no longer be allowed to drift along. Involvement in political action was called for. This was an overwhelming necessity. A victory for Hitler would deprive life of all meaning, not only for the intellectuals but for all of France.

Still, after Munich, there was no clear political path. On the contrary, everything was in a state of confusion. Nizan resigned from the Communist Party as a result of the Germano-Soviet pact. Colette Audry, who had felt deeply the agony of Republican Spain, went into semi-retirement from political life. Banned from the S.F.I.O. at the Royal Congress in 1938, she occupied herself with the colonial commission of the P.S.O.P. (*Parti Socialiste Ouvrier et Paysan*). But overcome by the hopelessness of the situation, she concluded that in view of the approaching war nothing could be done and that no one thing was more important than another. "No further independent revolutionary political activity was possible," she said.

Sartre was already thinking of the postwar period. He decided to take an active role in politics, "alone in the fray," and in this way lay the foundation for a new and authentic morality in which man would assume his condition by transcending it. For Sartre knew now that "men are the cause of everything and each individual is a whole man," that "we exist only if we act." Recognizing the effective solidarity that binds all men, he now intended to complete his speculative efforts by *praxis*. "Relation with the Other was no longer the question. What was important now was relation with others," as Colette Audry remarked.[7] It is impossible to be free alone. Such a freedom would be an abstraction because Others and History would manipulate it from outside. As Hegel said, "The individual cannot be free unless all are." Only action is liberating; it alone is the measure of man; it is impossible to remain a passive spectator.

Commitment, which was to be much discussed later (and was often criticized and commented upon with unimaginable incomprehension) as the basis of political morality, is therefore a conscious act, constantly called into question. It is the object of a choice. It follows from the

fact that man does not exist unless he is committed, that
to be uninvolved would be to let one's life be aimlessly
shunted about. This is what Sartre discovered at the time
of the Munich crisis. He never asked people to listen to an
interior voice proclaiming: "You must be committed." "As
though one could be otherwise. In other words, what was
first of all a judgment of fact was taken as a value judgment. It was thought that Sartre was condemning the
'ivory tower' when in fact he was saying, more radically,
that it was impossible." [8]

With the advent of the war and mobilization, and
above all the concentration camps, anti-fascist solidarity
became a reality. In *Bariona*, the unpublished play that
Sartre wrote for the prisoners of Stalag, an invitation to
the Resistance was easily discernible under the guise of
Christian mythology. Political realism consisted first of all
in treating a subject (a Christmas story) "that would be
capable of realizing the greatest possible union between
Christians and unbelievers." These were also the last words
of Bariona: "I am free. I hold my destiny in my hands. I
march against the soldiers of Herod and God marches at
my side. How free I feel, Sarah, free, ah, if you knew how
free I was! Oh joy, joy! Tears of joy!" [9]

When he returned from prison, Sartre resolved to join
with other anti-Nazis he knew to organize the Resistance.
With Merleau-Ponty, Simone de Beauvoir, Jean Pouillon
and others he founded the movement known as Socialism
and Freedom. Since the movement was made up of intellectuals who had no practical experience, it was soon
reduced to total impotence. The Communists refused to
cooperate and even helped spread the rumor that Sartre
was a policeman in the pay of the Germans. To avoid

pointless arrests Sartre decided to dissolve Socialism and Freedom. He joined Colette Audry who had been fighting since the beginning of the war with the Popular Front in Grenoble, in the early part of 1943. The Communists forgot their accusations, in fact denied that they had ever been made. Sartre therefore collaborated with them in the C.N.E. (Comité National des Écrivains), participated in meetings presided over by Paul Éluard and worked on *Lettres Françaises*.

These efforts were not motivated by a completely developed doctrine of commitment. For Sartre and Simone de Beauvoir, such commitment was absolutely necessary, but theoretically it was not totally exempt from Idealism. The plight of Orestes in *The Flies* shows quite clearly the ambiguity of this quest for freedom. Written in 1943, the play urges the French to put aside their regrets and throw themselves into the Resistance. It contrasts freedom with order. Orestes dreams of liberating his country, which is oppressed by Agistes, the usurper, and Clytemnestra. He finds that an abstract freedom without real choices is mere deception, that History is corporeal and weighs on one, that blood is frequently the price of progress. He can no longer feel himself apart from men and their History. "Others become the indispensable intermediaries between him and It." Orestes kills the tyrant and his accomplice and delivers his people, but instead of remaining to work with others to rebuild the country and complete what his gesture had only begun, he flees to solitude. Once again, he feels himself alien to his own people, or rather he resolves to be so. After staining the royal throne with the blood of the tyrant, he refuses to sit on it. If, as Jeanson wrote, Sartre chose to end his play with this "noble and distant attitude, could it not be because he saw the Resistance primarily as the personal adventure of each resistant and saw no other response to this trial of freedom than a kind of *heroism of the conscience?* I realize that after 1944 he spoke of total responsibility and the historical role of each individual. But if Orestes had really killed the usurper and his accomplice for reasons of historical responsibility, what sense are we to make of his flight?" [10]

In fact at this time Sartre conceived action as individual although in History. In *Being and Nothingness* man was described as free *in situ* in the world—an existant whose essence was precisely that he did not have one. Sartre wrote that "man loses himself as man in order that God may be born." [11] Only action permitted the birth of man. As the nothingness of being, the For-Itself was a perpetual projection outside of itself toward its pro-ject. As such, it was an artifact. Because he cannot be a thing in the way that an object is a thing, man defines himself only through action. He creates himself in this manner. Action is clearly assigned the role of "creating man, that creature who, even in the least of his acts, can never totally succeed in getting away from himself in his concern for the world." [12] Action is both presence to self and presence to the world; only action enables man to overcome his perpetual lack of harmony with himself. The whole last part of *Being and Nothingness* develops this theory as an answer to man's moral quest.

But the idea of *praxis* remained unclear, and many problems raised by the existing social structure were either badly handled or altogether missed. The question of class struggle, for example, was barely sketched in and often ignored. Relationship with others, which could have been the beginning of an analysis of class structure, was considered primarily from a negative point of view. "The essence of the relations between consciousnesses is not the *Mitsein**but conflict," Sartre wrote in *Being and Nothingness*. Of course, his analysis was intended to be descriptive rather than normative or exemplary. We cannot blame Sartre's ontology for its ethical omissions; the question of salvation was left suspended, as Francis Jeanson demonstrated in 1947. But we have a right to criticize *Being and Nothingness* for its ontological lacunae which later on would seriously limit the paths of freedom. Man remains solitary and must forge his own values and goals in total "abandon." Nothing and nobody can help him in his quest for liberty. The existence of the Other, which must be recognized as necessary, is aggressiveness. *No Exit*, staged for the first time in 1944, made no contribution to the philosophical problem.

However, after the Liberation, Sartre did not act like Orestes. He had no intention of letting himself be trapped anew in blind activity or a false aesthetic retreat. He proposed to be militant, among and with other men. In this respect his speculative thought lagged behind practice and political reflection. *Being and Nothingness* must be seen as only one aspect of Sartre's thought. The emphases on certain themes did not mean that everything was said once and for all. Much remained to be done. *Being and Nothingness* may be considered an expression of Sartre's Idealist period. In its last pages there is a counterbalance to this notion— an outline of a morality of responsibility, and Sartre's own

---

* *Mitsein* is a technical term used by Martin Heidegger in *Being and Time*. It means man's authentic existence with others. *Dasein ist wesenhaft Mitsein:* Human being is essentially communal.— B.M.

commitment. In Sartre's philosophy nothing is final, for the action it implies also constantly transforms.

They were determined not to transcend their condition as if it were an abstract, and thereby fail to take it seriously, so joining men's struggles; Sartre, Merleau-Ponty and Simone de Beauvoir "need have no fear that our choices or actions restrict our liberty, since choice and action alone cut us loose from our anchorage," Merleau-Ponty wrote. Among the future founders of *Les Temps Modernes*, Merleau-Ponty was perhaps most sensitive to the necessity of complementing freedom with *praxis*. At the end of *Phenomenology of Perception* he wrote: "Shall I make this promise? Shall I risk my life for so little? Shall I give up my liberty in order to save liberty? There is no theoretical reply to these questions. But there are these *things* which stand, irrefutable; there is before you this person whom you love; there are these men whose existence around you is that of slaves; and *your* freedom cannot be willed without leaving behind its singular relevance, and without willing freedom *for all*. Whether it is a question of things or of historical situations, philosophy has no function other than to teach us once more to see them clearly, *and it is true to say that it comes into being by destroying itself as a separate philosophy*." [13]

Notes

1 · Sartre, J.-P., in his preface to *Aden Arabie* by Paul Nizan (Paris, Maspero, 1960), p. 56.

2 · Beauvoir, Simone de, *The Prime of Life*, tr. Peter Green (London, Penguin, 1962), p. 32.

3 · *Ibid.*, p. 216.

4 · Sartre, J.-P., *Search for a Method*, tr. Hazel Barnes (New York, Knopf, 1963), p. 18.

5 · Sartre, J.-P., *Essai sur la transcendance de l'égo*, quoted by Simone de Beauvoir in *The Prime of Life*, op. cit., p. 183.

6 · Sartre, J.-P., *The Reprieve* (Vol. II of *The Roads of Freedom*), tr. Eric Sutton (London, Penguin, 1963), p. 277.

7 · Audry, C., *Connaissance de Sartre* (Paris, Julliard, 1955), p. 66.

8 · Pouillon, J., *Pour ou contre l'existentialisme* (Paris, Atlas, 1948), p. 60.

9 · These words must be read in reference to Goetz's speech at the end of *The Devil and the Good Lord* (New York, Vintage, 1960), where Sartre indicates the basis of a morality and a politics that are both human and possible.

10 · Jeanson, F., *Sartre par lui-même* (Paris, Seuil, 1955), p. 146.

11 · Sartre, J.-P., *Being and Nothingness*, tr. Hazel Barnes (London, Methuen, 1957), p. 615.

12 · Jeanson, F., *Pour ou contre l'existentialisme*, op. cit., p. 39.

13 · Merleau-Ponty, M., *Phenomenology of Perception*, tr. Colin Smith (London, Routledge & Kegan, 1962), p. 456.

Part I

❧ ❧ ❧ ❧ ❧ ❧

A THIRD WAY WITHOUT

A THIRD FORCE

1945—1950

Chapter

I

THE HUNTERS OF MEANING

SINCE THEORY cannot be separated from practice, *Les Temps Modernes* aimed to be both an expression and a means. "We had dreamed of this review since 1943," wrote Sartre. "If the Truth is one, I thought we must, as Gide said of God, seek it not elsewhere but everywhere. Each social product and each attitude—from the most private to the most public—are its allusive incarnations. An anecdote reflects an entire era as much as the substance of a political constitution. We would be hunters of meaning, we would speak the truth about the world and about our own lives." [1]

Thus *Les Temps Modernes* was intended to be an enterprise of unmasking, and it was to unmask in order to change. A journal form seems the best instrument for this task since it can be in touch with passing events and be detached enough to reflect on them. A journal also offers a chance for dialogue and criticism that a book does not give.

As a collection of writings, it can express the meaning of an age, indeed almost the entire body of knowledge of that age. Provided its editors are vigilant, nothing is foreign; it can give an account of everything.

In September, 1944, a committee of directors was named: Raymond Aron, Simone de Beauvoir, Michel Leiris, Maurice Merleau-Ponty, Albert Ollivier, Jean Paulhan and Jean-Paul Sartre. André Malraux did not want to participate and Camus refused because of his responsibilities at *Combat*. The first issue of *Les Temps Modernes* appeared in October, 1945.

In the beginning *Les Temps Modernes* was concerned with laying its foundations. So much had been upset, destroyed and condemned by the war that it was now imperative to look at some problems from new angles. In order to *make* history it was first of all necessary to define the role of the intellectual. A definition was needed that would be both objective and normative, since it would not only strive to reveal the true character of reality but accept it and transcend it as well.

The writer, as writer, is responsible. Some did not believe this, even when they collaborated with the Germans and were shot or punished for their articles, books and opinions. Words can be a weapon and, in any case, they are not neutral. "There are words as murderous as gas chambers, Jaurès' assassin was armed with words, words drove Salengro to suicide. In the case of Brasillach, there was no question of a mere 'offense of opinion'; his denunciations, his advocacy of murder and genocide constituted a direct collaboration with the Gestapo." [2] If literature is an influence and part of men's lives, there is no good reason to excuse Brasillach under the pretext that all he did was talk and write. Simone de Beauvoir refused to sign a petition asking clemency for Brasillach and criticized Camus for doing so. For the editors of *Les Temps Modernes,* political solidarity was of first importance.

"The writer is neither Vestal nor Ariel," said Jean-Paul Sartre. "He is 'in the thick of it'; whatever he does has far-reaching consequences. If in certain ages he has used his art to forge sonorous inanities, even that is a sign. . . . The ruling classes encouraged him to fritter away his talent for fear that he would lend his support to revolutionary forces. In no case can the writer carry out his mission without making sacrifices." [3]

This decision for voluntary action and the criticism of prewar writers, whose indifference was in reality a cover-up for complicity, was dealt with at more length in a series of articles Sartre published between February and July of 1947, under the title *What Is Literature?* This book might be considered a reasoned synthesis of the ferment of ideas brought on by the war and the founding of T.M. The writer has only one means of influencing the course of events: to write. "The 'committed' writer is aware of the identity of word and action; he knows that the act of unmasking brings about change and that one only acts in this way in order to change things." [4]

What Is Literature? defines writing as a multidimensioned activity and puts a strong emphasis on its political import. Sartre's analysis was concrete (he argued for total incarnation), and was rooted in real situations and as history obliged. The existentialists of *Les Temps Modernes* stood by this position. They strove to give content to action in order to avoid a formalism which they had always rejected as well as a pseudo-morality of action for action's sake which would in the final analysis become mere gestures and games.

It is not the same thing, Sartre remarked, "if one gets drunk alone or leads nations." Nor can we do first one and then the other, as Montherlant, St. Vincent de Paul, Kant and Casanova recommend. Nor is it any longer possible to treat political questions as a branch of morality or proclaim, in season and out, abstract truth.

Freedom was on trial and sides had to be chosen. The editors of *Les Temps Modernes* resolutely chose democracy, a dynamic democracy that would bring about changes in the economic and social structure of France. From the beginning, collaboration and conservatism were severely condemned. The idea of "revolution by law" was also vigorously rejected as being "an attempt merely to prolong what it pretends to abolish." [5]

The existentialists of *Les Temps Modernes* were asked for their reasons. The disrepute in which certain people held them, calumnies circulated by much of the press, and accusations that their philosophy was anti-humanistic constrained them to justify themselves, to prove that their attachment to democracy was sincere. In a word, they had to demonstrate that existentialism was indeed a humanism. This they tried to do, but it was by no means an easy task. The most substantial part of their work—psychology and certain metaphysical analyses excepted—underlined the desire to be of the world of men in order to change it. This position was not rationally deduced; it had been thrust on them by the war. But outside of Marxism they were hard put to find convincing arguments for it. The philosophy of history, which influenced *What Is Literature?* to some extent and colored their specifically political

discussions, was not up to the level of existentialist ontology. They described freedom as individualistic, but political action was taken as social and therefore collective.
To go from ontology to a realistic political ethic required
a bridge: namely, morality. But Sartre's promised treatise
on morality never appeared. The existentialists' statements
of moral justifications were brief, taking the forms of lectures, articles and essays, and scarcely amounted to a coherent system. Moreover, their authors were very critical
of them later on.

If man must in effect create his own values in lonely
isolation, if we cannot choose for others and others cannot
choose for us, then morality is an exclusively individual
matter. But this the existentialists could not admit. That is
why Sartre added another perfectly universal criterion to
that of free choice—truth. In *Existentialism and Humanism*[6] moral judgment is defined first of all as a judgment of
truth. Bad faith and incoherence are condemned in the
name of logic. It is true that one cannot will freedom by
denying it at another level. But why may not certain
choices be based on error? Why is coherence better than
incoherence? Because it is a question, Simone de Beauvoir
said, of knowing "whether man wants to live and under
what conditions";[7] life is not a search for being but freedom without exterior justification. "Thus just as life becomes identified with the will to live, so freedom always
appears as a movement of liberation." [8]

Since man is not and can never become a thing, freedom alone must be the end and means of human life. Thus
an aesthetic approach was condemned; pure artistic activity
is mere mystification, contemplation, a vain effort to become God. To live authentically man must act, and all

action, we might paraphrase Husserl, is action for something. A man who wants to be a free man among other free men cannot act inhumanly. The adventurer for whom action is a mere means of feeling alive no longer acts, but play acts, and he will end sooner or later as a mercenary, an instrument of those who pay him.

This was a weak justification for democratic politics. The foundations of socialism cannot be laid outside of class, and freedom cannot be defined concretely without taking man's *work* and needs as an absolute point of departure. A morality of *praxis* cannot be deduced from an analysis of the liberty that haunts the hearts of all men without taking social and historical factors into consideration. For Sartre the conflict of consciousnesses was the basic conflict, the model which other forms of conflict imitated. Class struggle, insofar as it was pertinent, was nothing but a manifestation of the original struggle of consciousnesses. At this point Sartre did not understand class struggle to be an irreconcilable conflict of material interests. In other words, the existentialist analysis of this period made no specific affirmation of the social phenomenon.

The existentialist position was still highly moralistic and Simone de Beauvoir now admitted that, like Sartre, she was still insufficiently liberated from the ideologies of her class. Sartre and Simone de Beauvoir professed a universal ethic in which an unlimited freedom served as the form of a concrete freedom that was sketchily defined.

On the other hand, Merleau-Ponty, who was searching for a nondogmatic Marxism, referred to historical man and based his analyses on the philosophy of history. He hoped in this way to verify the Marxist theory of the proletariat. Sartre said that he often saw Courtade, Hervé and Desanti.

Merleau-Ponty was responsible for the political direction of *Les Temps Modernes*. "A Marxist *faute de mieux*," and sensitive to the weight of reality, he was at this time *the* politics of the journal.

The general orientation of *Les Temps Modernes* was clear in spite of many contradictions. In the first place, Sartre came around to Merleau-Ponty's way of thinking. Also, his attachment to the revolutionary party, like Simone de Beauvoir's, was sincere, although his motives were muddled. To be sure, Sartre wrote some unsettling lines: "Just as anguish cannot be distinguished from a sense of responsibility so despair is one with the will; true optimism begins with despair: the optimism of a man who expects nothing, who knows that he has no rights and that nothing is due to him, who rejoices in relying upon himself alone and working for the good of all." But, more importantly, he affirmed: "Class struggle is a fact; I accept it unreservedly." [9]

Although contradictory to the first, Sartre's second affirmation took objective primacy because the editors of *Les Temps Modernes* wanted to fight exploitation, colonialism and war as well as the systems which engendered such evils. The journal was revolutionary for the wrong reasons (or rather, it had difficulty in justifying its position and relating ontological analyses to political positions). But it was nonetheless revolutionary. One thing kept Sartre from floundering in reformism: He had always conceived political life as a conflict and had decided to take part in that conflict. [10]

One chose the side of freedom of the person and the socialist revolution. Allegiances were determined in terms of this twofold cause. But after the extraordinary Manicheanism of the Resistance the situation was more confused. In the beginning *Les Temps Modernes* did not fully approve of any party. The first issue of the journal argued that the M.R.P. was only a front for traditional reactionaries, that the S.F.I.O. was hesitant and fearful, that the Communist Party had lost the proletarian spirit and become an organization whose tactical gambits were more inspired by the necessities of Russian politics than by the interests of the working class.

Class struggle was disguised. The moment of history was equivocal. Said Merleau-Ponty: "Everyone is a realist, an opportunist, a tactician." And he asked: "Is there therefore no choice between becoming cynics or rogues?"

Les Temps Modernes came into being to abolish this alternative. Its whole *raison d'être* can only be understood in this perspective. In this respect the manifesto published on the back cover of the first collection of articles from the journal, edited by Merleau-Ponty and Sartre, is very significant. It was a proclamation of general political intentions and made an attempt to define the role of the intellectual on the new Left: "This collection, like the journal whose name it bears, proposes to fight against that pathetic and prophetic spirit which is becoming more widespread every day and demands of our contemporaries blind decisions and painful commitments. It is not true that the world is divided into two empires of good and evil. It is not true that we cannot think without weakening nor be strong without talking nonsense. It is not true that good intentions justify everything, nor that we have the right to the opposite of what we want. The comedy of history, the switching of roles and the frivolity of the actors do not prevent us from discerning a clear enough course of action, provided only that we take pains to know what is going on rather than nourish phantasms, and provided that we distinguish anguish from anxiety and commitment from fanaticism."

What then was this "clear enough course of action" that the editors of *Les Temps Modernes* proclaimed possible? And how was it related to Marxism, since the editors intended to eventually "rediscover Marxism on the road of present-day truth and in the analyses of our times"? [11]

Notes

1 · Sartre, J.-P., "Merleau-Ponty," *Situations*, tr. Benita Eisler (New York, Braziller, 1965), p. 244.

2 · Beauvoir, Simone de, *Force of Circumstance*, tr. Richard Howard (New York, Putnam's Sons, 1964), p. 22.

3 · Sartre, J.-P., "Présentation des *Temps Modernes*," *Situations II* (Paris, Gallimard, 1948), pp. 12–13. The article also appeared in the first issue of *Les Temps Modernes*, October, 1945.

4 · Sartre, J.-P., *What Is Literature?*, tr. Bernard Frechtman (London, Methuen, 1950), pp. 123 ff.

5 · Pouillon, J., "Un Souhait étrange: la révolution par la loi," *Les Temps Modernes*, No. 1, October, 1945, p. 190.

6 · Sartre, J.-P., *Existentialism and Humanism*, tr. Philip Mairet (London, Methuen, 1948). This was a lecture Sartre gave to answer a number of particularly absurd criticisms of existentialism. While indicative of his thinking at that time, it was a slight work and cannot be considered as a definition of existentialism. The polemical tone of the text—which was not intended for publication—shows that it was not an exposition of a "doctrine." The importance later given to it seems due to the laziness of those critics who were hesitant to read *Being and Nothingness* and were happy to be able to attack Sartre easily and with a good conscience after having read less than a hundred pages.

7 · Beauvoir, Simone de, *The Ethics of Ambiguity*, tr. Bernard Frechtman (New York, Philosophical Library, 1948), p. 15.

8 · *Ibid.*, p. 32.

9 · Sartre, J.-P., "A Propos de l'existentialisme, mise au point," *Action*, No. 17, December 29, 1944.

10 · See Fields, Belden, *An Examination of the Ontological Foundations of the Political Theory of Jean-Paul Sartre*, 1961, p. 5: "Sartre is a revolutionist and views all political activity as conflict."

11 · Merleau-Ponty, M., "Pour la vérité," *Les Temps Modernes*, No. 4, January, 1946. These remarks are found on pages 578 and 600.

Chapter

2

A CLEAR ENOUGH
COURSE OF ACTION?

Les Temps Modernes soon took a specifically political line. "To place oneself on the political plane is to abandon one's individualistic position; it is to reach out to others and transcend the present in terms of the future." [1] This political action was conceived of outside of bourgeois idealism, which it had often condemned. It consisted first of all in fighting capitalism, the aftereffects of the war and the uncertain peace which followed. It was a program for peace against power politics.

As early as December, 1945, the journal came out against General de Gaulle's political ideas. Analyzing the elections of October 21, 1945, an unsigned article asked whether or not France would "once again and inopportunely have recourse to the expedient of a savior." The political situation was described as serious. "The Weimar Republic has taught us how mass democracies fare when they are led by strongmen," the article continued. The charter of the C.N.R. had not been put into practice and consequently the Resistance ceased to exist as a separate entity. New cleavages appeared. *Les Temps Modernes* had no desire to encourage a confusion that would make it seem Rightist. In June, 1946, it parted company with Raymond Aron and Albert Ollivier. Sartre and Merleau-Ponty, concerned about the rising tide of the cold war, stated that in case of war (and probably the death of the soul) they would side with Russia. Aron was clearly on the side of the United States. Although he had little sympathy for Gaullism during the Resistance, he was soon to accept a position with the national committee of the R.P.F. Albert Ollivier, an editorialist with *Combat* in the days of its glory, quickly sided with the Gaullist Union, became an enthusiastic member of the R.P.F. and edited *Le Rassemblement*, the official organ for the party. Simone de Beauvoir pointed out that "the words Right and Left had resumed their old meanings, and the Right was gaining ground; in May the M.R.P. had gained a majority vote."

But during the first year analyses took precedence over positions. Pierre Uri described the economic and financial situation; Louis Cleyssac denounced the disorder of the Constituency. But it was obvious that the journal was still trying to find its way. International problems were discussed in articles on the United States and Roumania. When the journal published a statement by Tran Duc Thao, an Indochinese who had been arrested for security reasons by the French police, it did so to "provide a platform for the guilty party without taking responsibility for his views." Like most reviews at the time, *Les Temps Modernes* published many articles on war and Nazism.

Then, in December, 1946, the journal suddenly came out with an extraordinarily clear and violent position on the war in Indochina. The first editorial to be signed "Temps Modernes" dealt with this problem. Here is a sampling of the opinions expressed: "In view of the snatches of news that come from Indochina and the headlines we read in newspapers, dominated as they are by a senile warrior fury or a pitiful embarrassment and always a sadistic taste for sensational news, only the words 'indignation' and 'refusal' can characterize what we feel." "If we are really driven to war, and if we really only have a choice between fighting and getting out, then by all means let us get out." "It is altogether unthinkable that after four years of occupation the French fail to recognize their image in Indochina, that they do not see in it the face of the Germans in France."

This was an important text. The journal attacked the government directly and across-the-board; it was the first time it had taken so clear-cut a position. Also, the colonial policy of *Les Temps Modernes* was to remain constant for nearly twenty years. If, as we shall see later, the journal changed its mind radically on many issues, it was from the beginning clear about colonial wars and defended the colonized against the colonizers without any ambiguity whatsoever. The editors were the first to see the importance of these questions for France and the French Left, the first to demand immediate and unequivocal independence. They did not discover colonialism only with the Algerian war. Already in December, 1946, colonialism was one of the most frequently discussed themes. The journal published several texts on military operations and repressions; in March, 1947, it released another editorial on this subject, once again opened its pages to Tran Duc Thao, and J. Pouillon, in the May, 1947, issue, denounced the "list-lessness" of the National Assembly.

But there were other pressing questions as well. We shall see in the following chapter how the existentialists reacted to the problems raised by Ramadier's 1947 decision to "dismiss" the Communist ministers, and by the politics of the French Communist Party and Russia. The United States also became a preoccupying concern.[2] Simone de Beauvoir discussed this subject in her *America Day by Day*,[3] the tone of which contrasted markedly with the articles Sartre sent to *Combat* and *Figaro* from the United States in January, 1946. Sartre had written with sympathy although he had certain criticisms and reservations. Simone de Beauvoir denounced the "semblance of democracy that was disappearing day by day in America" and "the despotic tendencies which were emerging with greater impudence." The issue of January, 1948, inaugurated a series of discussions on the Marshall Plan and protested the purges in Washington. In July, 1948, an editorial clarified the journal's policy on the United States and the Marshall Plan: "It is necessary to speak about American racism and implicit fascism." The Marshall Plan is not an evil in itself, the editorial explained, but it certainly aims to establish the political imperialism of the United States. "The best way to fight it is not by rejection; rather we must accept it but change its meaning. Refusal would signify our acceptance of power politics and the cold war. We must make American aid the affair of the proletariat and take up arms not against American aid but against the imperialist use of this aid." The editorial opposed the course of the war and the stratification of positions, and it made an overt attempt to define the framework for a politics of coexistence between the two powers.

Confronted with both the cold war and the war in Indochina, *Les Temps Modernes* tried to elaborate a politics of peace. Disagreeing with Camus, who feared that this played into the Communists' hands, the senior editors signed a petition in December, 1948, for negotiation in Indochina together with Claude Bourdet, André Breton, Jean Cocteau, Abbé Pierre, A. Mandouze, Vercors and others. In the February issue Étiemble called for French neutrality. In the final analysis, Sartre declared in a radio speech, "we do not believe that man is a mere refusal. If we do no more than say No we will inevitably be led to violence. It is not a question of frenetically destroying one of the two power blocs. On the contrary, we must organize ourselves between them. And this should not only be a French effort, but European and world-wide. Let us not wait for help and encouragement; let us take the initiative." [4]

Evidently these policies did not please everyone. They were often maliciously attacked. "Existentialists are idiots. Existentialism represents the triumph of idiocy and filth. It is 'excrémentialisme,' " declared *France au Combat*. Sartre received insulting letters that clearly indicated the hatred (and intellectual incompetence) of his adversaries. "Mr. Jean-Paul Sartre, you are an ignoble individual. I can't understand why a man of your stamp hasn't been stoned. You are a blockhead and an ass." Or: "How much are they paying you?" And: "You are no Frenchman." Another wrote: "You are an ignoble individual. If the crematory ovens of Germany still existed they would serve well to rid us of people like you." [5]

The reaction of the bourgeois press reached a paroxysm of violence after a radio discussion of Gaullism by the editors of *Les Temps Modernes.* Alarmed by the growing influence of the R.P.F. and its success in the municipal elections, Sartre, Bonafé, Merleau-Ponty, J.-B. Pontalis and Simone de Beauvoir answered the pro-Gaullist arguments and painted the R.P.F. as a reactionary party with fascist tendencies. Sartre even joked about de Gaulle's mustache, which he compared to Hitler's. The Gaullists had never much liked Sartre. *Liberté et Esprit,* a journal for the intellectuals of the R.P.F., commissioned Jacques Robichon to write regular anti-Sartrian columns. Sartre was accused of being "ignorant" and was called "a man with curdled blood who lacks vitamins." Monnerot opined that the French novel should free itself of his influence. Existentialists were dubbed "pundits of Merleau-Ponty." Pierre de Boisdeffre, in one of the most virulent attacks against both *Esprit* and *Les Temps Modernes,* exclaimed: "The mild dreamers at *Esprit,* enamored of an uncontrollable and complacent progressivism, wildly applaud even the least significant of Maurice Thorez's speeches, sit squinting in the Café de Flore and at night dream about Simone de Beauvoir. The success of the latter's *The Second Sex* among perverts and neurotics of all stripes prevents J.-M. Domenach from sleeping at nights. In the face of this psychoanalytic rot in the Anglo-Saxon style we can only pine for the ancient glory of France." [6]

It was clearly a highly unpopular radio program. Two years later, Claude Mauriac reminded his readers that Sartre tried to "dishonor [the Gaullists]. (In fact, the comparison of de Gaulle and Hitler had been in bad taste but should have only really distressed those low enough to stoop to that kind of humor. . . .) The writers of the

Left rely on their reputations to be permitted bad faith and stupidity. . . . A. Camus deceives himself while Sartre deceives others." [7]

The same program led to a break between Sartre and Aron, who was already writing for the *Figaro*, and seriously disaffected Malraux. The program sponsored by *Les Temps Modernes* would soon be suppressed by Schumann, who succeeded Ramadier in November, 1947.

The editors persevered in their struggle. They established contact with the opposition of the S.F.I.O. (Marceau-Pivert, Gazier). They met with those who had no party affiliation (Camus, Breton, Rousset) to discuss peace and the future of a socialist and neutral Europe. They signed, together with the editors of *Esprit*, a text favoring such a political program. But other breaks were occasioned by the split with Gaullism. Sartre no longer spoke to Arthur Koestler, author of *Arrival and Departure*. Koestler had said that "all things considered, Gaullism was the best solution for France." [8] Then Merleau-Ponty accused Malraux of confusing Trotskyism and Gaullism (although Malraux had been an anti-Trotskyite before the war).

The row was fierce and remained so during the first years of the cold war. *Les Temps Modernes* adamantly refused to make any concessions to the Western world. A preface signed "Temps Modernes" appeared in October, 1949, attacking the British Labor Party as "a modern form of English imperialism" which "with other sentiments, another ideology and, in daily life, a respect for freedom which is decidedly the only merit of 'democracies,' is the continuing bad joke of national socialism." The criticism was only aggravated by the repressive Anglo-American policy in Greece.

The two problems which would later assume such

great importance to the existentialists of *Les Temps Modernes* were now beginning to emerge clearly: Korea and
above all Algeria. Francis Jeanson, in *Esprit*, had already
appealed to his compatriots to recognize the Algerian
problem, although "no one was willing to admit that he
was sitting on a volcano." He denounced the "miserable
calculations and sordid combinations that persist in being
taken quite literally for the French policy in Algeria."
Jeanson was already on the side of those who "demanded
justice and humanity and who would fight to the death
to achieve them."

This was the battle at *Les Temps Modernes,* its editors'
day-by-day struggle against reactionary forces. They were
living proof of the political definition Merleau-Ponty gave
the group on January 1, 1946: "We must be careful that
nothing in our action contributes to impeding the rebirth
of the proletariat movement across the world. If there is a
strike, support the strikers. If there is a civil war, side with
the proletariat and let us do everything in our power to
prevent a conflict between the United States and Russia;
in a word, the effective policy of the Communist Party
must be to reconstruct with the proletariat. For the moment there is nothing else we can do. Let us simply follow
a policy of waiting, without illusions about expected results and without honoring it with the name of dialectic." [9]

The journal, it would seem, faithfully followed the
"effective policy of the Communist Party." It was just as
severe in its criticism of the postwar policies of the West
(indeed more severe in the case of the war in Indochina,
for example). At the same time, the existentialists continued to criticize many aspects of communism. Nonetheless,
while their political activity was directed against the Right

and the United States, they defined their situation with reference to the French Communist Party and Russia. They predicated a veritable "anti-imperialist" and "anti-reactionary" politics upon the transformation of the Communist Party and the French Left. It was, therefore, their relationship with the Communist Party that really constituted the specifically political and theoretical basis of their struggle.

Notes

1 · Beauvoir, Simone de, "Idéalisme moral et réalisme politique," in *L'Existentialisme et la sagesse des nations* (Paris, Nagel, 1948), pp. 66–67. Published in *Les Temps Modernes*, No. 2, November, 1945; No. 3, December, 1945, p. 555.

2 · Sartre had already published some strong criticisms of American political life in *The Respectful Prostitute*. See Sartre, J.-P., *Three Plays*, tr. Lionel Abel (New York, Knopf, 1949).

3 · Parts of this book were published in *Les Temps Modernes*, Nos. 27–31 (December, 1947–April, 1948). Jean Touchard remarked that "it is interesting to compare Simone de Beauvoir's book with *Clés pour l'Amérique* by Claude Roy, then a member of the Communist Party. Both books appeared within a few months of each other. Simone de Beauvoir is much harder on America than Claude Roy." See *Le mouvement des idées politiques dans la France contemporaine*, by Jean Touchard, R. Girardet, R. Rémond (Cours I.E.P., 1959).

4 · This speech was given in 1947 and reprinted in *Pour ou contre l'existentialisme* (Paris, Atlas, 1948), p. 189.

5 · *Ibid.*, pp. 182–85.

6 · Boisdeffre, P. de, "Témoignages en marge d'une enquête," *Liberté de l'Esprit*, Summer, 1949.

7 · Mauriac, C., "Pour un dialogue de bonne foi," *Liberté de l'Esprit*, February, 1949.

8 · Quoted by Simone de Beauvoir in *Force of Circumstance*, tr. Richard Howard (New York, Putnam's Sons, 1964), p. 140. She recounts in some detail the end of her friendship with Koestler on pp. 141 ff.

9 · Merleau-Ponty, M., "Pour la vérité," *Les Temps Modernes*, No. 4, January, 1946, p. 600.

Chapter

3

ONE CANNOT BE
ANTI-COMMUNIST,
ONE CANNOT BE COMMUNIST

In DISCUSSING the relationship between existentialism and communism, or more precisely Communist politics, we must be careful not to give too much weight to philosophical factors. Periods of philosophical *rapprochement* are not necessarily periods of political agreement and vice versa. Thus Sartre's quasi-alignment with Communist politics in 1952 was justified by a specifically existentialist ideology that borrowed little from Marxism or Leninism. On the other hand, the criticism of Russia and the position of the French Communist Party during the Hungarian Revolution in 1956 were determined by the principles of Marxism and socialism.

But it must be noted that although the existentialists did not always refer to class as a fundamental operational concept in the years following the Liberation, they never considered it unrealistic or outmoded. On the contrary,

Maurice Merleau-Ponty spoke of class as early as 1945,[1] and in the first issue of *Les Temps Modernes* Sartre used the terms "bourgeois class" and "working class."

Still, the existentialists rarely appealed to Marxism as a global system before the years 1953–54, with the possible exception of Merleau-Ponty who was to abandon it precisely then. In 1946 Sartre was in marked disagreement with materialism which he saw as metaphysics dissimulated as positivism. He rejected the dialectic of nature as absurd and took note of dialectical materialism only because it destroyed bourgeois idealism. But while he admitted the purifying aspect of Marxism and considered it a useful tool in the hands of revolutionaries, he thought it ontologically in error. Sartre rejected the analysis of superstructures and the theory of reflection. He considered Marxism liberating in its idealism but mystifying in its definition of man and truth; at least this was true of "scholastic Marxism" and "Stalinian neo-Marxism." Materialism is a philosophy of "things"; according to the Communist Party, history no longer has anything to do but read and follow. At that time Sartre urged the Communists, for the good of their revolutionary design, to adopt a new ideology. "We cannot indiscriminately form the young by teaching them successful errors. What would happen if materialism one day stifled the revolutionary project?" Sartre wrote in *Temps Modernes*. But no new philosophy was available; and even if it had been, the Communist Party and the working class would not have been ready to adopt it. Nor did the "Marxism without illusions, completely experimental and voluntary" that Merleau-Ponty wanted exist.[2] The majority of the working class remained attached to the Party and its old materialism. Sartre wrote in the same issue of the journal: "I know that the liberation of the working class is the only salvation for man." He then inquired: "Have I fallen into the unacceptable dilemma of betraying the proletariat in the name of truth or betraying truth in the name of the proletariat?"

Could it be otherwise for a group of revolutionary intellectuals in light of the Communist Party's claim of a monopoly on revolution? "The masses were behind the Communist Party; socialism could triumph only through the Party. Furthermore, Sartre was now aware that his connection with the Party entailed a radical re-examination of his life." [3] A bourgeois intellectual, he was cut off from his public which did not want to draw radical political conclusions from the crisis brought on by the war. Sartre saw his interest—the universality that all intellectuals try for—in harmony with that of the working class, the "universal class." His future and his values would necessarily be bound up with others; those who in his opinion realized those values badly and had been, in the beginning, absolute strangers to him. The confrontation between the Communist Party and the French existentialists was originally begun with the latter suffering from guilt feelings. It is striking to notice how Simone de Beauvoir saw the relationship between the Party and a revolutionary bourgeois. In *Le Sang des autres* she presented the Communist Party as a kind of forbidden paradise. It is normal for the worker, born to the proletarian class, to be a Communist; the Party is made for him; it is his only path to dealienation and liberation. On the other hand, the intellectual with a bourgeois background can never fully belong to the Party. He will always be something of an outsider, will always be capable of setting off in a different direction; his commitment lacks weight. But the proletarian is tough, and communism is his way of living freely. It is not for the intellectual. The intellectual, the enlightened bourgeois, suffers this useless passion since he is always aware that he can never be a Communist.

The same theme is found in Sartre's writings. In *Dirty Hands*, Hugo is a member of the Party, but he has never been fully accepted. Moreover, he had never known hunger. Just to the contrary, when he was a child he was forced to overeat. No real need led him to the Party; he chose it freely and gratuitously.

This way of presenting and experiencing things is revealing. It explains the Sartrian wing of existentialism vis-à vis the Communist Party. The latter is viewed from the outside as a bloc, as a possibility of liberation in which some individuals, with all the good will in the world, can never participate without bad faith. Moreover, the Party does not totally liberate even those for whom it was made. It alienates them too, but in a different sense. It engenders in its adherents a seriousness that Sartre compared to the manner of a café waiter.

In *Dirty Hands* Slick and Georges are portrayed as brutish. In *The Roads of Freedom*[4] the Communist leader Brunet plays at being responsible. At first his way might seem to be the best solution. But we soon see that history has left him behind. In a prison camp in 1941 Brunet's work is savagely compared to that of a curé by Sartre. In the unfinished fourth volume[5] Brunet becomes a machine, repeating the Party's Truth. But what he does not realize is that both Truth and the Party have changed. Henceforward he will live (and die) in debauchery and in accursed friendship with a renegade Party member.

This gives us some clue as to the relationship between the existentialists of *Les Temps Modernes* and the Communist Party. Sartre was an immediate threat to the Communists. "As soon as the calm seas of 1945 were past they attacked me," he wrote. "My political thinking was confused, my ideas were dangerous." [6] The kind of praise he received from *Action*, which noted Sartre's "extremely brilliant passage" in *Confluences* and pointed out that "his criticism develops side by side with Marxist analysis," was not to last long.

Still Sartre wanted to maintain an understanding, even a friendship, with the Communists. "Against the kind of Marxism professed by the Communist Party, he tried to safeguard man's human dimension. He hoped the Communists would make room for the values of humanism. And he tried, with the tools they lent him, to tear humanism from the clutches of the bourgeoisie . . . on the political level, he felt that Communist sympathizers should play a role outside the party similar to that played within other parties by the opposition, a role that combined support with criticism." [7]

All of this seemed possible just after the Resistance when the journals, Communist or not, exchanged editorialists and all the political Left was in broad agreement and even shared the same hatreds. Moreover, Sartre's contacts with Communist intellectuals led him to think that their differences were not serious. He met with Courtade, Ponge, Rolland, Kanapa (who had been his student), and wrote an article in the first issue of *Les Temps Modernes*. The Communist press supported *Troubled Sleep*, in which Sartre sympathetically portrayed a militant Communist. But the Party soon grew suspicious of the success of existentialism. The importance given the movement in the general press did not incline them to indulgence, and all the more since Sartre might corrupt Communist intellectuals by offering a substitute ideology to conservatives who were short on ideas. The latter were not beneath plagiarizing some of his analyses which they might interpret to suit their own purpose. The Communist attacks were at first discreet but soon became more intense; and one is aware that Communist vocabulary and imagery can be very vicious. Sartre, at first surprised, quickly perceived that the articles did not originate with "uncontrollable elements" in the Party. In *Entretiens sur la politique*[8] he tells how he tried to maintain dialogue without giving in on principles or relinquishing his right to criticize. The Communists answered him by charging that he was "in the pay of the American ambassador," that he was "defending a dying middle-class culture." In that era the Communist Party considered existentialism ideological enemy number one.

Sartre nonetheless tried to carry on discussion in an atmosphere of good faith. In an article he submitted to *Action*[9] he tried to clarify their divergencies and points of agreement and bring to a halt personal insults and criticisms. He was granted a few months' respite. But in June, 1945, Henri Lefebvre[10] wrote that he no longer imputed Sartre "with having been a disciple of the Nazi Heidegger," but nonetheless considered him an idealist, a subjectivist and a munitions maker against Marxism. From this time forward insults were the order of the day. *L'Humanité* adopted the habit of referring to the existentialists as lackeys of Gaullism (or American imperialism, depending on the context). In season and out, the Communists accused Sartre of "reducing men to animals as a philosopher, of playing into the hands of reactionaries as a politician, of being a decadent gravedigger as a writer and rotten as an individual." In *Existentialisme n'est pas un humanisme*, Kanapa suggested that Sartre was a fascist abcess. Nizan, about the same time, was treated by the Communist press like a "cop." Sartre decided to affirm some harsh truths and with Mauriac, Bost and Guéhenne signed a text protesting Nizan's ill-treatment. And he remarked in *Les Temps Modernes* that "the policy of Stalin's communism is incompatible with the honest exercise of the writer's trade."

When *Dirty Hands* appeared the Communist Party had a paroxysm. But the play was not intended to be anti-Communist, and in it Sartre put Hoederer, the militant Communist, on the side of justice against Hugo, the young individualistic bourgeois who had joined the Party. But, as Simone de Beauvoir explained, "the play seemed anti-Communist because the audience was on Hugo's side. Hoederer's murder was taken as an equivalent of the crimes imputed to the Cominform." The play seemed anti-Communist because both the bourgeois and the Communist Party wanted it to be. "For thirty pieces of silver and a mess of American pottage, Jean-Paul Sartre has sold out what remained of his honor and probity," wrote a Russian critic.[11] When the film based on the play was released the Party sent militants to picket the theaters. Nonetheless Sartre remained calm and protested that his polemic with the Communists was not like his conflict with the Catholics, that it was merely "a family quarrel" and if he had to choose between communism and the Church (or the R.P.F. or the U.S.A.) he would unquestionably choose the Communist Party.

Merleau-Ponty, for his part, was not subject to such

vitriolic attacks. Closer to the Party and lacking Sartre's dubious notoriety and embarrassing "disciples," he was in frequent contact with Communist intellectuals. Since he "was much better oriented in the ambiguous world of politics," he wrote the editorials signed "Temps Modernes" and elaborated a political line vis-à-vis communism in *Humanisme et terreur*.[12] But when the book appeared Merleau-Ponty was in his turn dragged through the mud. As regards communism Sartre may have had strong feelings, as we have described, but Merleau-Ponty was in fact in charge of the journal's political policy. Sartre admitted that he had little taste for political life. And Merleau-Ponty wrote that Sartre approved everything he wrote in advance.[13]

As early as January, 1946, Merleau-Ponty had defined a general policy. The middle class was floundering in its own contradictions and the proletariat was not strong enough to launch a revolution. Russia, even though she practiced socialism on an economic level, could not formulate an effective policy for the proletariat. Therefore, "in view of the facts, let us no longer tolerate equivocation," and "let nothing in our action interfere with the proletarian movement that is being reborn all over the world." [14] One had to follow the Party's policies without illusions.

But still one had to know why and how. Merleau-Ponty tried to establish a socialist politics (and a violence) "that would point to the future" and define it with respect to Stalinist communism. The series of articles on "the communist problem" entitled *Le Yogi et le prolétaire* began to appear in *Les Temps Modernes* in October, 1946.[15]

From the beginning the study was carried out in a

revolutionary perspective, for "any discussion from a liberal point of view avoids the problem since we are concerned with a country that has had and pretends to continue a revolution and liberalism excludes the revolutionary hypothesis." [16] The question "is not whether communism respects the laws of liberal thought, which it obviously does not, but whether the violence it exercises is revolutionary and capable of making men more human." Merleau-Ponty did not seek a moral solution. Instead he affirmed that all politics is immoral, that every regime kills or provokes wars. The important question is to know why this is so and what the results of this hesitant, erroneous, bloody and all too human politics would be.

The Communists did not invent terror; they found it already established. Anti-Communists "refuse to see that violence is everywhere." The critic of Soviet socialism is wrong insofar as he cannot suggest a valid replacement. Merleau-Ponty quoted Saint-Just: "A patriot is one who supports the whole Republic; whoever opposes in any way is a traitor." Subjective intentions must be disregarded; objectively speaking, those who were condemned in the Moscow trials had done a disservice to the Revolution. "Opposition is betrayal." But this truth must be modified and, as Simone de Beauvoir said, "Merleau-Ponty recalled that inversely traitors may only be opponents." It is not cowardice but on the contrary proof of good political judgment to choose a Russia which schemes and plots with history over the abstract kind of revolution that crumbled under Nazism.

This choice is valid on condition that the accompanying violence is transitory, only the growing pains of a new historical era. But the Russian proletariat was too weak to assume its role as a value-bearing class for humanity (Marx), and the proletariat itself has ceased to be the point of reference for Communist thinking. However, the difficulties of communism did not authorize the French Left to adopt a hostile attitude toward it. "Its difficulties are our difficulties," said Merleau-Ponty, and added that the real problem was to determine whether or not the Revolution could dispense with terror. But to side with humanism against terror would amount to abolishing every means of establishing such a humanism; for humanism is founded on collective production which historically in Russia has always given rise to terror. Marxism remained the only realistic philosophy of history. It was possible that the proletariat would recapture its central place, and in any case the proletariat still identified its lot with Russia. The role of the existentialists was therefore "to remind the Marxists of their original humanist inspiration," unmask the fundamental hypocrisy of Western democracies and "maintain intact, against all propaganda, whatever chances history might still have of becoming clear once again." [17]

Thus we can understand the attitude of *Les Temps Modernes* when the Communist ministers left the Ramadier government in 1947. "The Communist Party is threatening a general strike, all the while disavowing the political objectives this implies . . . *for want of principles and clarity* it is about to fail in the arena of class struggle after having failed in the arena of political unity . . . more than ever before the question must be asked: Is a minimal socialist politics possible today and if so what kind?" [18]

This appeal to clarity, principles and humanism would be the basis of existentialist politics vis-à-vis communism

until around 1950 when it adopted an anti-capitalist position very much like that of the Communist Party. It is in
this context that we must understand the journal's protest
against the Soviet camps. *Les Temps Modernes* urged a
"policy which does not require them to choose *their* de-
ported persons"; they did not forget the Greek deportees
and the massacres of the colonial wars. Denying that the
Soviet camps were economic institutions, they refused to
confuse communism and fascism. "We have the same values
as a Communist . . . we may think he compromises them
by embodying them in today's communism. The fact remains that they are ours, and that on the contrary, we have
nothing in common with a good number of communism's
adversaries . . . whatever the value of the present Soviet
society may be, the U.S.S.R. is on the whole situated in the
balance of powers, on the side of those who are struggling
against the forms of exploitation known to us. The deca-
dence of Russian communism does not make the class
struggle a myth, 'free enterprise' possible or desirable, or
the Marxist criticism in general null and void. From which
we do not draw the conclusion that indulgence must be
shown toward communism, but that one can in no case
make a pact with one's adversaries. The only sound criticism is thus the one which bears on exploitation and oppression, inside and outside the U.S.S.R and every political
position which *is defined* in opposition to Russia and lo-
calizes criticism within it as an absolution given to the capitalist world." [19] What the article said, in other words, is
that regimes should be judged as much by their intentions
as their actions and that Russia was, despite its crimes, on
the side of mankind's future. The existence of the camps
and the attitude of the French Communists, who pretended

that the penitentiary system was a Soviet achievement, were to be condemned. But, as Sartre told me in 1961, "That is no denunciation of socialism and it is quite conceivable that the beginning of the socialist era will be marked by a more or less lengthy and critical period of terrorism. Russian society merely interiorized the terror that was brought to bear on her. Still we have declared the fact inadmissible and we reacted very vigorously."

That is why Sartre did not conceal his sympathy for Tito's version of communism. He saw it as a human reaction against Stalinism. If Tito could thaw the Soviet glacier, Sartre was willing to bet on him.[20]

The implications of this attitude, strictly interpreted, are clear enough. Since the proletariat remained stagnant, and since the Communist Party, as its expression and guide, committed errors and crimes, the present task was, as Francis Jeanson was to say later and not without irony, to "address ourselves to the proletarians and teach them the true principles of a true revolution; but for this political power at least equal to that of the Party is necessary." [21] The S.F.I.O. could not furnish this power. To join the Socialist Party would be tantamount to "consenting to the politics of idiots." "Preferring not to see 'this struggle for recognition,' the struggle to the death of consciences and classes, the Socialist Party dreams of an impossible reconciliation and in fact can only preserve what should be immediately abolished." [22] As Sartre said, "In such an epoch as ours, in which there are various parties, each advertising itself as the Revolution, commitment does not consist in joining one of them, but in seeking to clarify the conception, in order to define the situation and at the same time to try to influence the different revolutionary parties." [23]

Sartre hoped for the advent of a socialist revolutionary party to increase the strength of the S.F.I.O.'s left wing and contest, restrain and threaten the all-powerful Communist Party.

Simone de Beauvoir fictionalized such a situation in *The Mandarins*.[24] The non-Communist but revolutionary Left edited *Espoir*, a journal that was read by the workers, and organized a political group called the S.R.L. Its aim was to prevent the Communist Party from treating people like things, to force it to accept the "minimal socialist policy" that Merleau-Ponty had spoken of, and to constrain the Communist machine by example and pressure. In the novel this plan failed; the Communist Party rejected the right wing of the S.R.L. and forced it into an anti-Communist position. Since the directors of the S.R.L. refused to go along with this, the movement disappeared.

This imaginary account is significant. Such a theoretical position on the problems posed by Russia and the French Communist Party could foretell a politics of this kind. In fact Sartre and some others tried it with the Rassemblement Démocratique Révolutionnaire (R.D.R.).

Notes

1 · Merleau-Ponty, M., "On Liberty," *Phenomenology of Perception*, tr. Colin Smith (London, Routledge & Kegan, 1962), pp. 434 ff.

2 · Merleau-Ponty, M., *Sense and Non-Sense*, tr. Hubert L. and Patricia Allen Dreyfus (Evanston, Illinois, Northwestern University Press, 1964), p. 124.

3 · Beauvoir, Simone de, *Force of Circumstance*, tr. Richard Howard (New York, Putnam's Sons, 1964), pp. 6–7.

4 · *The Roads of Freedom* comprises three published volumes: *The Age of Reason, The Reprieve* and *Iron in the Soul* (London, Penguin, 1963).

5 · Sartre, J.-P., "Drôle d'amitié,": the only part of the fourth volume of *The Roads of Freedom* (entitled *La Dernière Chance*) to have been published. See *Les Temps Modernes*, No. 49, November, 1949, pp. 769–806. In it we read such statements as: "I believe everything the Party says" (Brunet); "I never have an opinion; I expound the policies of the Party" (Charlais, a leader in the French Communist Party).

6 · Sartre, J.-P., "Merleau-Ponty," *Situations*, tr. Benita Eisler (New York, Braziller, 1965), p. 237.

7 · Beauvoir, Simone de, *Force of Circumstance, op. cit.*, p. 17.

8 · Sartre, J.-P., *Entretiens sur la politique* (Paris, Gallimard, 1949), Chapter 15 of the first interview: "Aventures et mésaventures des intellectuels Staliniens," pp. 70–78.

9 · Article published in *Action*, No. 17, December 29, 1944.

10 · Lefebvre, H., "Existentialisme et Marxisme, réponse à une mise au point," *Action*, No. 40, June 8, 1945.

11 · Beauvoir, Simone de, *Force of Circumstance, op. cit.*, p. 151.

12 · Merleau-Ponty, M., "Les Essais," *Humanisme et terreur: essai sur le problème Communiste* (Paris, Gallimard, 1947), xxvii, xliii, p. 206.

13 · *Ibid.*, p. 600.

14 · *Ibid.*, p. 13.

15 · These articles were reprinted in *Humanisme et terreur*.

16 · *Ibid.*, p. 13. The following four quotations are from the same source: pages 13, 4, 36 and 48.

17 · Beauvoir, Simone de, *Force of Circumstance, op. cit.*, p. 15. There is no doubt that statements of this kind greatly displeased Albert Camus, who was at this time becoming more and more anti-Communist.

18 · "En un combat douteux," editorial, *Les Temps Modernes*, No. 27, December, 1947, pp. 961–64. (Our emphasis.)

19 · Merleau-Ponty, M., and Sartre, J.-P., "Les Jours de notre vie," *Les Temps Modernes*, No. 51, January, 1950. In fact the article was written by Merleau-Ponty and published in *Signs*, tr. Richard McCleary (Evanston, Illinois, Northwestern University Press, 1964) as "The U.S.S.R. and the Camps," pp. 263–73. This editorial was written before *Le Figaro Littéraire* published a series of articles by David Rousset denouncing the Soviet camps—that is, before the matter became widely known to the public.

20 · See Sartre's preface to *Le Communisme Yougoslave depuis la rupture avec Moscou*, by L. Dalmas (Paris, Terre des Hommes, 1950).

21 · Jeanson, F., *Sartre par lui-même* (Paris, Seuil, 1955), p. 155.

22 · Pouillon, J., *Pour ou contre l'existentialisme* (Paris, Atlas, 1948), p. 83.

23 · Sartre, J.-P., *Existentialism and Humanism*, tr. Philip Mairet (London, Methuen, 1948), p. 59.

24 · Beauvoir, Simone de, *The Mandarins*, tr. Leonard M. Friedman (London, Collins, 1957).

Chapter

4

LE RASSEMBLEMENT DÉMOCRATIQUE RÉVOLUTIONNAIRE (R.D.R.)

THE R.D.R. WAS an important episode. The existentialists —and Sartre foremost among them—threw themselves for the first time into a concerted effort on behalf of the masses. Like other militants, they no longer addressed themselves to public opinion in general or intellectuals but attempted "to rediscover the great democratic tradition of revolutionary socialism." The R.D.R. "cannot nor does it wish to be anything unless it first of all refers to the working class." [1]

Jean-Paul Sartre participated fully in this experiment. He was responsible for the R.D.R. and his involvement was much greater than his later allegiances to various movements, including the Peace Movement. One might almost say that the party was the Rassemblement of David Rousset and Jean-Paul Sartre. But it would be ridiculous to say the the Peace Movement was Sartre's. Maurice

Merleau-Ponty also gave his allegiance, although he seemed primarily motivated by a reluctance to disavow Sartre. Merleau-Ponty did not believe in the R.D.R. and had quite different ideas about how protest against the Communist Party should be organized. "In order to live as closely as possible to the Communist Party, to force it to accept certain criticisms, we had, first of all, to be politically ineffective, so that they could envision another role for us," Sartre wrote later. "Merleau-Ponty was just their man. Solitary, without partisans or zealous disciples, his thinking always new and renewed, he had faith only in himself. The Rassemblement, on the contrary, however small it was and admitted itself to be, was counting on force of numbers." [2]

Merleau-Ponty never went to meetings of the executive committee, of which he was one of the founding members. But he continued to direct the journal.

The R.D.R. was founded in the beginning of 1948 by journalists and militants of the non-Communist extreme Left: Georges Altman, Jean Rous, Gérard Rosenthal and especially David Rousset, a former member of the International Communist Party (Trotskyite). Other members of that party also supported the founders of the R.D.R. When Sartre was asked to become part of the movement, he accepted. It seemed to him an effective way to give political life to his ideas. Torn between humanism and Communist practice, between the middle classes and the proletariat, he felt at home in a movement that took up a position midway between the S.F.I.O. and the Communist Party.

In February, 1948, a tract was distributed in Paris. It was the committee's appeal for the Rassemblement Démocratique Révolutionnaire. "Between the rottenness of capitalist democracy and the weaknesses and flaws of a certain kind of social democracy and the limitations of communism in its Stalinian form," it proclaimed,[3] "we think that a party of free men for revolutionary democracy is capable of giving new life to the principles of freedom and human dignity by relating them to the struggle for social revolution." It attacked both Stalinist methods and "capitalist democracy, which is no more than the reign of the rich and the slavery of the poor." The appeal thus completed Marx's phrase: "Proletarians and free men of the world, unite!" The initial committee was composed of writers and journalists (including David Rousset, Jean-Paul Sartre, Paul Fraisse of *Esprit*, and six editors from *Franc-Tireur*), four deputies, militants from the working classes and syndicalists.

The committee's appeal was published in the press. Claude Bourdet reviewed it favorably in *Combat* but Georges Altman, one of the editors of *Franc-Tireur*, contrasted it with the Third Force and called for the formation of a grand alliance, of a world-wide assembly of revolutionary democrats. *Le Monde* greeted it with sympathy because "the committee's appeal has great nobility . . . and the men who compose it are deeply sincere." During a press conference on March 10, 1948, at which the principal speakers were Sartre, Jean Rous and David Rousset, the movement was described to forty-eight journalists in these words: "The R.D.R. is above all a rallying point for all the militants of Leftist parties"; "liberated from the monolithic spirit," it intends "to organize democracy" and "put Europe in the forefront of the cause for freedom." The first general assembly of the R.D.R. was held on March 12, 1948. Rous declared: "We need fifty thousand members from Paris within a month!" "And why not?" asked *Franc-Tireur*.

But who did the R.D.R represent? Some thousand Parisians who attended the first meeting, a group of ex-militants from the P.C.I. and some well-known intellectuals like Sartre. It had the sympathy of *Combat* because Bourdet and Camus were very close to the movement and sometimes wrote in its official organ, *La Gauche*. It also had the much-appreciated support of *Franc-Tireur*,[4] many of whose non-Communist editors like Bernard Lefort, Jean Ferniot, Georges Altman, Charles Ronsac and Jean Rous belonged to the Rassemblement. The Jeune Republic, a Christian leftist organization, and some militants from the S.F.I.O. also joined the movement.

The R.D.R. hoped for a large audience, first of all because of its structure—it did not claim to be a new party but simply a "gathering." That is to say that it permitted its members to belong to other parties, and hoped in fact for the support of an important number of Communist and S.F.I.O. socialists.

But little could be expected from the Communist Party. Fearing that the Rassemblement would recruit from circles not in sympathy with them, the Communist leaders immediately launched a violent campaign. The R.D.R., Pierre Hervé charged, "did not want to offend Malraux and Aron or disappoint the S.F.I.O. ministers, Jules Moch and Lacoste."[5] And Jean Kanapa averred that "when the R.D.R. says that organisms of contact should be expressly created (expressly!) to regenerate 'the democracy of the working class,' the militant worker is tempted to reply: 'Organisms of contact? They have already been created. Your friends are in charge of them and they sent us the C.R.S.'"[6]

All bridges between the R.D.R. and the Communist Party were soon burned when the latter chose to call David Rousset and Jean-Paul Sartre agents of the government and Wall Street. Nor were things much better with the S.F.I.O. In the beginning there was some hope of influencing a minority in the Socialist Party; Marceau-Pivert looked upon the movement sympathetically. But the majority took a firm stand and warned that anyone who subscribed to the Rassemblement would be excluded from the S.F.I.O.[7] The socialist separatists of the A.S.R. (Action Socialiste Révolutionnaire, born of a split in the S.F.I.O.'s left wing) condemned the confusion reigning in the R.D.R., of which the working class would be the victim. When the A.S.R. held a rally on March 11, 1948, only two members (Dechezelle and Tomazzi) were sympathetic to the Rassemblement. Nonetheless, some 15 to 20 percent of the A.S.R. gave their allegiance to the R.D.R. Gilles Martinet, then the leader of the Partie Socialiste Unitaire, "gently reminded" Georges Altman that socialism cannot be rethought *with* but *against* Jean-Paul Sartre, and that "to combat communism 'in its Stalinist form' one must profess communism under another form." [8]

But the leaders of the R.D.R. certainly weren't doing this. The political line of the Rassemblement was clarified during 1948. It saw itself as a vehicle for "two classes, the proletariat and the middle classes, and not therefore as essentially Marxist in structure . . . but its existence and its necessity mark the inadequacy of the parties and perhaps point to a change in the paths opened up by history." [9] In any case, the R.D.R. wanted to be "a meeting place of all Leftists who rejected the Caesars and supreme saviors." [10] Consequently, it battled against Gaullism and Stalinism.

Gaullism is "unaware and criminal." And, as David Rousset pointed out, Stalinism had nothing to do with socialism. In *Entretiens sur la politique* and in many articles and speeches, Rousset insisted often and at length on the social oppression that was rampant in Russia and the Communist definition of alienation. Nonetheless, the Rassemblement remained friendly toward the Communist Party and hoped to work with it while preserving its liberty and its right to criticize the Party's methods and goals. Its declared intention was to reintroduce democracy on all levels. "Our first goal," said Sartre in *La Gauche*, "is to link revolutionary claims with the idea of freedom." The second issue of *La Gauche* asked a question on its front page: "Palestine, South Africa and Czechoslovakia. But where are freedom and democracy?"

As a means of promoting "democracy without catechism," as Camus called it in the fourth issue of *La Gauche*, the R.D.R. called for international peace, Sartre for a federated union of a neutral Europe, and Bourdet for the end of "the politics of suicide" in the French colonies. On the last, positions were already clear cut. *Entretiens sur la politique* had declared that "we must speak out clearly about the territories overseas," urged independence for them, and charged that "the French ruling class did not understand that this century marked the end of colonialism." Sartre, speaking to a Moroccan audience on November 18, 1948, said: "Those who oppress you oppress us for the same reasons."

All these planks could be found in the R.D.R.'s projected program, which also proposed "to do everything to prepare the workers for the direct management of business."

What means did the Rassemblement have to carry out this program as well as be the bad conscience of the Communist Party? Its influence was relatively important from the beginning, primarily because of the renown of some of its leaders and the support of certain journals. What did it represent on the specifically militant level? It is difficult to furnish statistics, but the report presented to the executive committee on January 29 and 30, 1949, by Théo Bernard gives some indications. At the time the R.D.R. numbered some 1900 members, though this refers only to those who had officially submitted their names to the executive committee, and it is possible that the real number was somewhat higher. From Paris alone there were more than 736 members in August, 1948, and it had risen to 830 by December.

By age, membership broke down as follows: 25 percent under twenty-five; 45 percent between twenty-five and forty; and 30 percent over forty years old. Seventeen percent were manual workers and 33 percent union members. Sixty-five percent of the militants did not belong to other political organizations. The administrative office had three full-time executives and two secretaries.

The movement's financial status was always precarious and meetings were poorly attended. An administrative report showed that only about 25 percent of the members in the Paris region came to the meetings. The organization was almost everywhere very defective.

Sartre and his political friends headed a relatively weak and poorly structured organization with a diffuse but rather large audience,[11] a political line based upon a "positive neutralism" in foreign as well as domestic affairs, and with enemies attacking from all sides. Under such conditions what could be done?

Franc-Tireur sponsored an open forum over several days—entitled War and Peace—at which Camus spoke about organizing a movement for European peace. David Rousset spoke in the same vein, and André Breton called his article "Peace by Ourselves." Later, Sartre, refusing to choose between Russia and America, said that in this day the will for peace could not be separated from the revolutionary and democratic will.[12]

R.D.R. held a day of studies on December 13, 1948, which was advertised as a "democratic initiative in the struggle for freedom by invitation of the Rassemblement Démocratique Révolutionnaire." David Rousset, Jean-Paul Sartre, André Breton, Albert Camus, and other outstanding writers such as Richard Wright, Carlo Levi, Georges Altman, Claude Bourdet, Gérard Rosenthal, Simone de Beauvoir and Abdallah Ibrahim, called for an "internationalism of spirit."

Four thousand participants gathered in the hall and *Franc-Tireur* estimated that two thousand had to be turned away. The speakers dealt with internationalism, peace, a socialist Europe and unity.

The press campaign had been well organized. *Franc-Tireur* later published the principal interventions of the foreign writers. Except from the point of view of unity, it was an unquestionable success. *L'Humanité* referred to it as "an anti-Soviet meeting organized by a clique of intellectuals whose showy generalities and literary slogans scarcely dissimulate a deliberate acceptance of the capitalist regime." [13]

In January, 1949, R.D.R. launched a petition for peace in Indochina and called for negotiations with Ho Chi Minh. The petition was highly successful and a headline in *La Gauche* for February 11, 1949, read: "The people of all of France are against the dirty war." A number of meetings were organized about this theme.

Then the R.D.R. prepared an "International Day for Resistance to Dictatorship and War" which it sponsored with different French and foreign unions and organizations. The rally was to be held on April 30 in Paris, the same day that the World Congress of Partisans for Peace met. The leaders of the two groups met on April 16 with less than positive results: Rousset condemned the two military blocs and Casanova (from the head office of the French Communist Party), who represented the Partisans for Peace, directed his attack against the Atlantic Pact but refused to condemn an eventual Oriental Pact.

Once again *Franc-Tireur* gave a lot of coverage to R.D.R.'s position as in general to the non-Communist Left. For several days they devoted a full page to the "International Day for Resistance to Dictatorship and War." On April 14, David Rousset spoke about the "peace of free men," and on April 18, Édouard Depreux expressed agreement with the sense of the meeting.

On April 30, the large amphitheatre of the Sorbonne was filled for the morning meeting, and that evening, 10,000 persons were at the Vélodrôme d'Hiver. The non-Communist Left attended en masse since the Seine federation of the C.G.T.-F.O. had given its consent, as had the A.F.L. and the C.I.O. representing American organizations.[14] The Seine federation of the S.F.I.O. was present in equally large numbers. Sartre did not attend. He was doubting the efficacy of the R.D.R., and was beginning to suspect that Merleau-Ponty had been right. He was afraid that such a manifestation would encourage anti-communism. The presence of Americans and the date (the eve of May Day) cast doubt on the intention of the meeting. With Merleau-Ponty and Richard Wright, Sartre wrote a letter explaining his absence. The meeting was in fact pro-American. One speaker even praised the atomic power of America as an aid to peace.

A party of intellectuals at the R.D.R. began to sing the praises of America. Altman, in *Franc-Tireur,* exalted "the union civilization" of the United States. The unity of the movement was beginning to be seriously compromised. The majority of its leaders systematically sought alliances with the Right. This was soon to paralyze the R.D.R. and heralded its demise. David Rousset, who had already said that the Communist regime "represented the fiercest social reaction since the disappearance of Nazism," now affirmed that "the Atlantic Pact was not a measure of war." [15]

Sartre continued to defend an intransigent neutralism and declared himself always against the Atlantic Pact and for the neutralization of Europe.

In the meetings of the Rassemblement, Sartre reproached Rousset for moving too far to the Right. His friends questioned the financial management of the movement and Rousset's efforts to procure money from the American C.I.O. Sartre provoked the calling of an extraordinary congress on June 30, 1949, at which time he criticized sharply the orientation and conception of the April 30 rally. Violent debates had raged earlier when on the occasion of elections in March, 1949, the R.D.R. had let it be understood that it would be preferable to vote for the socialist S.F.I.O.

On October 15, Francis Jeanson officially announced that Sartre, "extremely disillusioned," had given his resignation to the R.D.R. On October 21 his resignation was official. "After a fairly brilliant beginning," wrote *Le Monde* on October 27, "the R.D.R. fell asleep. Dissensions seemed to weaken it still more. The departure of Mr. J.-P. Sartre is striking evidence of the movement's present inability to overcome its internal quarrels."

A few militants of the Rassemblement tried unsuccessfully to salvage it. For Sartre it was all over. The position he and Merleau-Ponty took on the Soviet camps[16] was very different from Rousset's, who wrote a series of articles for *Le Figaro Littéraire* in November, 1949, much to the pleasure of the bourgeois press. (*Franc-Tireur* had refused to publish them.)

Sartre's period of neutralism seemed virtually over and as a practical matter the cause has failed utterly. In the 1951 elections not a single neutralist candidate was elected despite some apparent sympathy for their position. Their intellectual influence failed to become a political reality. Sartre wrote that "Circumstances [had] merely appeared to be favorable to the association. It answered an abstract need defined by the objective situation but not any real need among the people. Consequently they did not support it." [17]

Cries in the desert, alignment with the Communist Party, a gradual tendency to the Right—there were no issues left for neutralism. The R.D.R. did not succeed in establishing a position between the Communist Party and the bourgeoisie. In the end the cold war, against which the movement proposed to fight, got the best of the R.D.R.

Notes

1 · Sartre, J.-P., Rousset, David, and Rosenthal, Gérard, *Entretiens sur la politique* (Paris, Gallimard, 1949), p. 159.

2 · Sartre, J.-P., "Merleau-Ponty," *Situations*, tr. Benita Eisler (New York, Braziller, 1965), p. 261.

3 · As the S.F.I.O. moved toward the Right, the R.D.R. became more severely critical of it and sought ways to fill the void that it created on the Left.

4 · *Franc-Tireur* then had a circulation of some 300,000, with a relatively large readership among the working class.

5 · Hervé, P., "Les Honnêtes Gens de la famille," cited in *Entretiens sur la politique, op. cit.*, p. 145.

6 · Kanapa, J., "Ces Messieurs et les mineurs," cited in *ibid.*, pp. 145–46.

7 · After the S.F.I.O. convention in July, 1948, the R.D.R. became openly critical of the Socialist Party, as indicated by an article by Georges Altman in *La Gauche*, No. 4, July, 1948, entitled "Après le Congrès Socialiste: nous sommes épouvantés."

8 · Martinet, G., "Parti ou rassemblement," *La Bataille Socialiste*, March 19, 1948.

9 · In *Entretiens sur la politique, op. cit.*, p. 41.

10 · Altman, G., "Ce Vieux Mot usurpé par les politiciens," editorial in the first issue of *La Gauche*, the official organ of the R.D.R., May, 1948.

11 · When Raymond Aron said that the working classes showed little interest in the R.D.R., Sartre answered that "just because the proletariat is not behind the R.D.R. doesn't mean that they have gone over to the R.P.F." See Aron, R., "Réponse à Jean-Paul Sartre," *Liberté de l'Esprit*, June, 1949.

12 · Sartre, J.-P., "La Paix pour refaire le monde," *Franc-Tireur*, December 10, 1948.

13 · Hervé, P., "La Clique de ceux qui ont rejeté en bloc la révolution," *L'Humanité*, December 15, 1948.

14 · Walter Reuther spoke at the meeting.

15 · Rousset, D., *The Nation,* New York, April 9, 1949.

16 · See "The U.S.S.R. and the Camps," *Signs,* tr. Richard Mc-Cleary (Evanston, Illinois, Northwestern University Press, 1964). In his "Reply to Albert Camus," Sartre raised the question of the camps again. "What is scandalous," he explained, "is that they were created by a socialist regime. That is why our denunciation of them should under no circumstances play into the hands of the anti-Communists who are already too happy to have found a proof that they would have invented had it not existed." See "Reply to Albert Camus," *Situations, op. cit.,* pp. 69–107.

17 · Unpublished notes cited by Simone de Beauvoir, *Force of Circumstance,* tr. Richard Howard (New York, Putnam's Sons, 1964), p. 177.

Part
II

❦ ❦ ❦ ❦ ❦ ❦

REVOLUTION AND WAR

1950–1956

Chapter

5

THERE IS THIS WAR TO FIGHT

IN 1950 THE SITUATION grew increasingly more serious. *Les Temps Modernes* had discovered the Soviet camps, massacres in Madagascar, war and repression in Vietnam, and McCarthyism. "How could we not smell the stench of the bourgeois cadaver? But how could we publicly condemn slavery in the East without abandoning our own exploited? Could we permit ourselves to work with the Party if it meant putting France into chains and surrounding it with barbed wire? What should we do? Should we mercilessly strike out at those giants to both the Left and the Right who wouldn't even feel our blows? This was a solution of despair. Merleau pushed it for lack of a better one. I didn't see any other solution either, but I was worried. We hadn't budged an inch; the 'yes' had simply changed to 'no.' In 1945 we said: 'Gentlemen, we are everybody's friend, and above all, the friend of our dear C.P.' And five years later: 'We are the enemies of all, the only privilege of the Party is that it still merits our severest judgment.' Without even speaking of it, we both had the feeling that this 'high-altitude' objectivity wouldn't take us very far." [1]

Then the Korean war broke out. At that time some intellectuals, including Merleau-Ponty, were much more impressed by the risk of war than by the necessity of taking strong positions. Apparently he felt at that time that the political period being over, the time of war begun, there would be nothing more to say.[2] He went from one threshold to another. As world war became more and more possible, the danger of absolute violence increased. Merleau-Ponty believed that Stalin thought war was inevitable. Russia was no longer a country of bloody socialism; it was an imperialist country like the others. "History had definitely perverted its course. It would continue paralyzed, deflected by its own waste, until the final fall."

Sartre had the opposite reaction. In an interview in March, 1961, he said, "for myself and some of my friends it was the end of idealism. In tactics there was no difference between politics and war, and even in war one must stay with his political party. The Korean war was not a Communist tactic. Quite the contrary. It was a trap into which the North Korean armies fell. We discovered then that the cold war could become a very hot war. With a certain amount of idealism we thought we could choose what we loved and preferred. The non-Communist Left was kept in the background by the Communist Party, but it did not want to go over to the other side. It found itself in no man's land, which is what had depressed the generation of 1945. From 1950 on we understood that there could be no question of choosing what we might most like;

our perspective had to be much broader. We had to side with those who took risks, those who were interested in peace, and therefore with the Soviets."

At the end of 1950, *Les Temps Modernes* fell silent. There were few political articles. Sartre later explained that there was no reliable information on Korea, Mac-Arthur's intentions, the Chinese lobby or Syngman Rhee. What was certain was that the North Korean army had attacked first—but at the time *L'Humanité* denied this version. Sartre said that they had discredited themselves by deliberately lying.

Merleau-Ponty was silent. The journal had lost its political direction. The other editors remained very close to the Communist Party. Dzelepy, in particular, wrote violently anti-American articles almost every month. "In short," said Sartre, "during the interregnum between 1950–52 a vessel without a captain by itself recruited officers who would save it from perdition." [3] But in reality the failure to abandon the Communist Party during those years in itself brought one terribly close to the chesslike French politics, since the Party itself was totally isolated.

The journal's political direction floundered until July, 1952. [4] In fact, individual decisions had already been made. Merleau-Ponty felt that he had been misled and thought of retiring. Sartre, on the other hand, worked on the problems of history, dialectics and action. He gradually abandoned the idea of writing a book on morality to follow *Being and Nothingness* as he became more and more convinced that "the moral attitude appears when technical and social conditions render positive forms of conduct impossible. Ethics is a collection of idealistic tricks intended to enable us to live the life imposed on us by the poverty

of our resources and the insufficiency of our techniques." [5]
Sartre was preoccupied with economics and psychoanalysis,
disciplines which involved him in the history of humanity
and the history of individual man.

Merleau-Ponty reacted to the difficult situation by
planning to forsake the Party. Sartre, however, decided to
explore the notion of *situation*, to discover the material
determinants and roots of man, and by discovering them,
to eventually take them upon himself and transcend them.
Sartre's "moral" period ended with *The Devil and the
Good Lord*.[6] In an uncertain time, this play took on considerable importance. It was not, as some pious souls would
have us believe, "a slap in Christ's face" administered by an
author "haunted by God's corpse." It is a serious work that
defines humanist morality and politics. Goetz, the hero,
first seeks absolute Evil. But absolute Evil is pure nonbeing
and an impossibility. So then Goetz wants to become a
saint. He would be absolute Good. But "Good without
Evil is a Parmenidian being, that is, Death." [7] For "either
morality is a fairy tale or it is a concrete totality which
achieves a synthesis of Good and Evil." Good and evil are
not separable and we must accept the fact that we are evil
in order to become good. Goetz learns how to assume full
responsibility for his actions; and he comes to know that
we only act with men against other men. Anarchy is resolutely rejected, and pure negation is condemned. The
play, when compared to *The Flies*, shows how much
Sartre's thinking had changed since the Resistance. Unlike
Orestes, Goetz stays with his people to the end. Instead of
waiting for a perfect alternative, he chooses in terms of
that "broader perspective." The evolution is clear—one
takes history upon oneself, *praxis* has become collective.
Political realism breaks in, as in Goetz's last tirade: "The

kingdom of man is beginning. A fine start! Nasti, I told you I would be hangman and butcher. . . . Never fear, I shall not flinch, because I know no other way of loving them. I shall give them orders, since I have no other way of obeying. I shall remain alone with this empty sky over my head, since I have no other way of being among men. There is this war to fight, and I will fight it." [8]

In short, Jeanson wrote, "the itinerary followed by Goetz seemed to exhaust all possible forms of idealism." [9] It demonstrated that morality can be defined only in terms of concrete *praxis*, commitment to history, attention to the demands of the real situation.

For some time yet the political articles of the journal would be signed by E. N. Dzelepy or I. F. Stone. Claude Bourdet was the only member of the team to take a clear-cut position. But the editorial committee was soon changed. The new members, Marcel Péju and Claude Lanzmann, were in agreement with Sartre's new ideas and hoped to work in close collaboration with the Communist Party.

During 1952 Sartre identified himself unreservedly with the Communists, who were searching out intellectuals to join in protesting Henri Martin's arrest. (Martin was a sailor who had been imprisoned for distributing tracts against the war in Indochina.) He was a member of the Committee for the Liberation of Henri Martin and used this occasion as a way of allying himself practically with the Communist Party. "Circumstances had convinced him that the only path still open to the Left was to find a way back to unity of action with the Communist Party. . . . Sartre had reached the same point as Goetz: He was ready to accept a collective discipline without denying his own liberty." [10]

On May 28, 1952, the Communist Party organized a

demonstration against General Ridgway, the American who had just been named head of SHAPE and who was held to blame for repressive policies in Korea. The demonstration was violent and the police intervened brutally. The next day the Communist newspapers were seized, and militants, including Jacques Duclos, were arrested. The Party was accused of spying for the Soviet Union. A general strike of protest on May 4 failed, and the whole right-wing press rejoiced.

Sartre, then in Italy, returned quickly to Paris. He later wrote: "These sordid childish tricks turned my stomach. There may have been more ignoble ones, but none more revealing. An anti-Communist is a rat. I couldn't see any way past that and I never will. . . . After ten years of ruminating, I had come to the breaking point, and only needed that one straw. In the language of the Church this was my conversion. In 1950, Merleau too was converted. . . . Our slowly accumulated disgust made us realize in one instant the horror of Stalinism, on the one hand, and that of one's own class on the other." [11]

In July, 1952, the first part of *Les Communistes et la paix* appeared. The article was violent, mordant, spiritual. But the ferocious attack Sartre launched against the Pinay government was not its most important aspect. *Les Temps Modernes* was in the habit of denouncing capitalism. Shortly before an inquiry entitled "Do We Have a Democracy?" had drawn conclusions scarcely flattering to the Fourth Republic. The colonial policy in Tunisia had been roundly denounced in March, 1952. But there was something new in the analysis of the Communist Party. The article began with a bitter criticism of Georges Altman and the moderate Left. Sartre argued that it was no longer possible to maintain an even balance between the horrors of the two blocs. He raised the concrete problems of the working class and its alliance with the Communist Party, as well as the May 28 demonstration against the war. "We cannot go against the working class without becoming the enemy of men and of oneself . . . and at all costs we must not count on the liquidation of the Communist Party," he wrote.[12] Further, "the working class still recognizes itself in the forced trials which the Party institutes in its name." The working class had had a bloody history, a history of oppression and deaths. The bourgeoisie had hoped the working class would see the errors of its ways and rally to them in spite of their record of exploitation. Sartre wondered "whether the 'incurable vice' the Communist Party is accused of is not simply the particular nature of the proletariat." He concludes that the Communist Party is the *necessary* and *exact* expression of the working class. To fight the Party even partially is to declare oneself an enemy of the proletariat, an enemy of humanism and an accomplice of the imperialism which risks war—indeed, implicitly or explicitly, seeks it. The struggle for peace and for an eventual humanism must be carried on in collaboration with the working class and its party—i.e., in the Soviet camp, since it is "the Soviet Union [that] wants peace and proves it daily."

A turning point had been reached. The breach between Merleau-Ponty and Sartre deepened, and there was a break with the neutralist extreme Left. The journal was soon to lose the services of René Étiemble. Étiemble found it intolerable that Sartre, in the interests of peace, "could cooperate closely with men who were making a profession of hating, ridiculing and organizing pogroms against the

Jews." [13] Nor could he accept the journal's preference for Claude Roy—"who learned everything he knows about dialectical Marxism from Maurras . . . a Stalinist-Nazi who plays at being a Bolshevik"—over himself. Étiemble, who still agreed with the pre-1950 positions of *Les Temps Modernes*, did not want to be associated with what he considered to be a betrayal of these positions and refused to join "the watchdogs of the Communist Party." He and Sartre parted company. The quest for unity of action was off to a bad start.

Notes

1 · Sartre, J.-P., "Merleau-Ponty," *Situations*, tr. Benita Eisler (New York, Braziller, 1965), p. 269. Reprinted with permission. English translation copyright © 1965 by George Braziller, Inc.

2 · Sartre confirms in the same article that Merleau-Ponty had told him then that the review should be quiet on politics.

3 · *Ibid.*, p. 285.

4 · At this time Sartre published the first part of his *Les Communistes et la paix*.

5 · Unpublished notes cited by Simone de Beauvoir in *Force of Circumstance*, tr. Richard Howard (New York, Putnam's Sons, 1964), p. 199.

6 · Sartre, J.-P., *The Devil and the Good Lord*, tr. Kitty Black (New York, Vintage, 1960).

7 · Sartre, J.-P., *Saint Genet: Actor and Martyr*, tr. Bernard Frechtman (New York, Braziller, 1963), p. 186.

8 · Sartre, J.-P., *The Devil and the Good Lord*, *op. cit.*, p. 149.

9 · Jeanson, F., "La Conduite humaine selon Jean-Paul Sartre," *Lignes de départ* (Paris, Seuil, 1963), p. 159.

10 · Beauvoir, Simone de, *Force of Circumstance*, *op. cit.*, p. 261.

11 · Sartre, J.-P., "Merleau-Ponty," *Situations*, *op. cit.*, p. 287. Reprinted with permission. English translation copyright © 1965 by George Braziller, Inc.

12 · Sartre, J.-P., *Les Communistes et la paix*, in *Les Temps Modernes*, in No. 81, July, 1952, p. 5. The following three quotes are from the same source, pages 49, 6, and 12.

13 · Étiemble, R., *Hygiène des lettres*, Vol. III of *Littérature dégagée (1942–1953)* (Paris, Gallimard, 1955), p. 148. Étiemble stopped collaborating on *Les Temps Modernes* in October, 1952. The text in question was a "Lettre ouverte à Jean-Paul Sartre sur l'unité de mauvaise action," which had already appeared in *Arts*, July 24–30, 1953.

Chapter

6

AN ANTI-COMMUNIST IS A RAT

IN 1952 SARTRE did not follow the classic logic elaborated by the non-Communist Left in 1948: "Thesis: One demonstrated the government's degradation, its crimes against the working class, and showed that the Communist Party was right. Antithesis: One revealed the vileness of the Politburo and its mistakes and showed how it, too, had injured the masses. Conclusion: One dismissed each on equal terms and indicated a middle course, citing the Scandinavian countries as support. In Merleau's view, I had developed only the thesis part. He was still hoping, without too many illusions, that the antithesis was yet to come." [1]

But it never came. Sartre joined the Peace Movement and went to Vienna for the World Congress for Peace in November, 1952, to lecture in the company of Communist delegates. He wanted to presage "future agreements by setting this tiny example: an agreement with the Communists which in no way affected our freedom of judgment." [2]

Sartre presumed that this attitude would be natural to the so-called committed writer. It was the logical political extension of his commitment. The "Reply to Albert Camus" demonstrates Sartre's thesis.[3] To Camus, still protesting against Manicheanism, denouncing the method of authority and radically questioning the new character of the Soviet revolution, Sartre tendered a vigorous reply. Francis Jeanson had accused Camus of a "certain ineffectiveness of thinking" and of understanding nothing about Marxism. Sartre was even more severe. Camus, he said, is not the brother of the downtrodden; he offers humanity no reasons for living. On the contrary, he flounders in solitary and catastrophic thought and has become "the Chief Prosecutor in the Republic of Hearts and Flowers." [4] "If we are tired, Camus, then let us rest, since we have the means to do so. But let us not hope to shake the world by allowing it to examine our fatigue."

In the final analysis, Sartre's whole answer was an appeal to efficacy, a thorough attack upon irresponsibility, idealism and subjectivity. Sartre's letter was political. The book that had provoked Jeanson and Sartre, *The Rebel*, was metaphysical and moral.

The basic orientation remained the same: We must accept our times and act to change them. History is not written in a reasonable heaven which directs its course; it is men who make it. "If a child died, you blamed the absurdity of the world and this deaf-and-blind God you created so that you could spit in His face. But if the child's father was a laid-off worker or an unskilled laborer, he reproached men. . . . From Malraux, from Carrouges, from twenty others, you borrowed some idea or other of the 'deification of man,' and while you condemned mankind, you stood next to it but outside its ranks." For Sartre it is impossible to break ranks; "the problem is not to know history's objective but to *give* it one." At that time, for the committed writer to give meaning to history meant to prevent the threatened end of mankind, to fight for peace side by side with the Communists.

This is what it means to abandon idealism: to cease saying no to everything, to cease dreaming of a proletariat in absolute conformity with one's own wishes, to cease hoping for an ideal communism born of a few proclamations to the working class and cleansed of Stalinism. The existentialists of *Les Temps Modernes* refused "to assist phlegmatically in the (even momentary) defeat of those who one day might be able to give reality its true meaning." For it would be "primarily a defeat of the workers and only secondarily of Stalinism," Jeanson wrote in *Esprit*. And since the proletariat was considered the only class capable of effecting a radical change in history, it would also be a defeat of the values for which *Les Temps Modernes* stood.

For four years the positions of Sartre and the journal did not change. The second part of *Les Communistes et la paix* appeared in the October–November, 1952, issue and the third part in April, 1954. Meanwhile, in a reply in *Les Temps Modernes* to Claude Lefort, Sartre clarified his conception of the Party's relationship to the masses. These three texts give a good indication of the journal's attitude toward the Communist Party as well as French political life in general.

"In France today," Sartre wrote, "only the working

class is equipped with a doctrine. It is the only class whose particular interests are the interests of the nation. A great party represents them, the only one to have made it part of its program to safeguard democratic institutions, re-establish national sovereignty and defend the peace, the only one to concern itself with democratic rebirth and the increase of buying power; the only one, finally, that is *alive*, that literally crawls with life while the others crawl with worms. And you ask by what miracle the workers follow most of its advice? I would pose the opposite question and ask what prevents them from following it all the time. The answer leaves no doubt: If the proletariat is showing signs of exhaustion, it is because it has been overcome with the anemia of the nation." [5]

Sartre analyzed the French situation. From 1910 to 1913 production had increased by 30 percent. Then it remained at that level. Agriculture had not been modernized and the farmers were not able to buy enough. Only the managerial class, as usual, consumed enough. "Prices are so arranged that we stay together." Sartre saw the fundamental vice of the French economy in the dispersion of enterprise—there were too many small producers and businessmen. Moreover business, large and small, was not modernizing. Plant equipment was decrepit and the cost of production was enormous. Consumption fell off as a result. "Have our capitalists read *Das Kapital*? To avoid crises they cut off competition, organized under-production, and reinvested their profits abroad. Thus they have created a depressed economy out of fear of depression." The bourgeoisie preferred stability to progress.

What caused this situation? In 1848 and in 1871 the bourgeoisie, seeing its true face, understood the magnitude of the proletarian threat. The workers revolted and the bourgeoisie reacted by terror and repression, turning the class struggle into a civil war. The worker was exploited everywhere, but he was massacred in France. France was deprived of a strong socialist democracy. The working class became increasingly alienated, and from 1871 on it felt irremediably rejected from the national community. Henceforward the workers relied on themselves alone: "They had only wanted to become *something*, but condemned for being *nothing*, they took revenge by becoming *everything*." "The working-class secret is that they consider the French bourgeoisie a gang of criminals."

In these conditions of war the bourgeoisie could only fear the exploited. It was well aware that a developed proletariat could bury capitalism. Moreover, statistics (Sartre cited those of 1906) showed that the worker had more children than the employer. It is impossible to "integrate" the working class; their blood had scarcely dried. "How can the terrifying ascendancy of the proletariat be prevented?" By keeping the farmer in the country, preaching Malthusianism and limiting technical concentration so as to retard social thinking? "Since the progress of capitalism was leading to its downfall, it became necessary to stop progress." The bourgeoisie did not try to produce more, nor did it hire more labor. Just the contrary. It wanted to produce as cheaply as possible so that fringe benefits would be as high as possible, and it increased its administrative staff to determine how to do it. Politically, Sartre explains, the plan was not without interest: The proletariat did not grow and a middle class was formed to act as brake. "Malthusianism made its point: a backward agriculture, a profitable middle class and a deprived proletariat—this guaranteed social stability." Big business surrounded itself with smaller industries as "a guarantee of security." It mystified the worker by creating inflation to cancel the increases in salaries. It even influenced proletarian organizations and encouraged schisms by compartmentalizing categories, creating a worker "elite" and setting the middle classes against the proletariat.

Stifled by economic and social Malthusianism, the wheels of French society continued to turn but more and more lifelessly.[6] The proletariat was sick—"an idle employer makes a tired proletariat." And "all things considered—Malthusianism and misery, high prices and rearmament as well as the Marshall Plan—to reject the politics of the Communist Party is to accept the government's." [7]

The Party's politics must, therefore, be accepted. Why? Because the future of democracy is in the hands of the working man and the Communist Party is the party of the working class. None of Sartre's group would have denied the first of these affirmations. Neither Merleau-Ponty, who asked whether a working class still existed, nor Claude Lefort.[8] But the second was contested. The whole second part of *Les Communistes et la paix* affirmed that the Party spoke for the working class, that the two could not be separated and that to attack one was to attack the other. The Communist Party is the organization of the proletariat *as class* and is therefore a distinct party; its vision is explicitly Marxist. All of the articles in the series attacked constantly those who pretended to talk about "a proletariat in itself," separate from its party, or those who saw the Communist Party as an obstacle to the freedom of the working man. If the proletarian did not always follow the Communist Party, explained Sartre, it is not because Communist politics disgust him, but because he is disgusted by all politics. This is the result of the unhappy state of French society.

Claude Lefort attacked this conception of the Party. His argument was simple and consisted in rejecting the Leninist theses. Sartre answered that "*today* the masses needed the Party," that "it was an instrument of mediation between men." He criticized Lefort's "spontaneity" and repeated that it made no sense to pretend that a bureaucracy rules the proletariat.

"It is in fact not a question of showing that the Party dictates its opinion to the masses. The Party is distinct from the masses only insofar as it is the union of the masses. By this union they create their identity and in terms of this identity they will decipher the *situation* of class in society and its present position in the secular struggle they carry on. The Party forms the social framework of the workers' memory; it is a sketch of their future; the organ of their action; the permanent bond which fights against their massification; it is the *perspective* within which the proletarian can situate himself in society and in his turn make objects of those who take him for an object; it is a tradition and an institution." [9]

This analysis of the Party rests upon the conviction that one cannot get out of a "serial," a passive addition of the individuals who constitute it, except with the help of a previously constituted group that is capable of "de-serializing" it. A class can only be partially defined as a group, as proletariat, to the extent that there is another group that acts upon the "seriality" of that class.

The Party does not rise directly from the class, in which case it would be subject to it. That is why Sartre condemned the lessons in direct democracy that many Leftists took upon themselves to give the Party. At best, they were ineffective and founded on an analysis that ignored social realities; at worst, they contributed to the "serialization" of the class. However, Sartre now thought that the analyses put forth in *Les Communistes et la paix* were inadequate. They were "dated as soon as they were written" because of the economic and social evolution in France and more especially because of the end of Stalinism. The Stalinist edifice, with its labor camps and terror, was at least coherent. With the end of the Korean war, the necessity for brutal choices diminished. With the death of Stalin a system that could not in any case replace true politics collapsed. Unable to promote a genuine policy of de-Stalinization or reinstate the preceding system, Stalin's successors, confusedly supported by both dictatorial and liberal principles, finally ran aground in Budapest. The fourth part of *Les Communistes et la paix*, which never appeared, was in a sense "Stalin's Ghost," an article Sartre published after the Hungarian uprising. The evolution of the international situation, the relatively peaceful coexistence that followed the Korean war and the inadmissible intervention in Hungary made Sartre's analyses of 1952–53 irrelevant.

Moreover, he now recognized that *Les Communistes et la paix* had theoretical weaknesses. "During a time when the only problem was what prevented the group from becoming 'serialized,' the party represented only itself. This raises the following problem of whether it is possible to conceive of democracy in the party without revolutionary movements. The party in a nonrevolutionary period is a party in expectation. It must both mobilize and demobilize (in order to wait). It is comparable to the Church's problem when it became evident that the kingdom of God was not imminent. Thus a party in expectation can only be judged by its action; it is not in itself legitimate. It is only legitimate if it acts as it should. That is why there can be no *real* representatives of the proletariat in a time of expectation or in a dictatorship like Stalin's. An analysis of the notion of legitimacy is what was lacking in *Les Communistes et la paix. . . .* In France at the moment the Party itself has become a 'serial.' " [10]

However, Sartre did not change his position toward the Communist Party appreciably until the Hungarian revolt. In February, 1956, in the journal he attacked Pierre Hervé, who had criticized the Party in his *La Révolution et les fétiches,* accusing him of criticizing from the outside, of having fallen into idealism, reformism and ineffective humanism. Marxism is a "culture in itself," but it is no longer alive. For "borne on by history, the Communist Party manifests an extraordinary objective intelligence; it is rarely wrong; it does what must be done; but its intelligence —which is confused with *praxis*—is not often incarnated by its intellectuals."

"Men of my age are well aware of this fact," Sartre added. "Even more than the two world wars, the all-important thing in their lives has been a perpetual confrontation with the working class and with the ideology of the working class which afforded them an irrefutable vision of the world and themselves. For us, Marxism is not merely a philosophy. It is the climate of our ideas, the environment that nourishes them, it is the movement of what Hegel calls the Objective Spirit."

For four years, therefore, Sartre remained close to

Communist politics. How could there fail to be agreement between the Communist Party and *Les Temps Modernes* when Sartre recognized the "Party [as] the movement which unites the workers by preparing them to take power?" [11]

A friendship was born between the Communists and Sartre. The kind of relationship Sartre had with the Italian Communist Party now became possible with the French Communist Party as well. At the Vélodrôme d'Hiver Sartre shared the platform with Jacques Duclos. *L'Humanité* forgot its former attacks and at the time of the Vienna Congress noted that the Congress gave Sartre a standing ovation.

Sartre, for his part, forgot the quarrels of the past. He forbade a revival of *Dirty Hands* in Vienna because it recalled too many bad memories, especially since the German version was much more anti-Communist (did the translator intend this?).

To be sure, *Les Temps Modernes* took the liberty of criticizing details. Thus Sartre labeled Kanapa a "cretin" for having called Colette Audry and the editors of *Les Temps Modernes* "Blumian revisionists," "intellectual cops," and the like. In July, 1956, a note signed "Temps Modernes" protested the fact that Auguste Lecoeur was wounded by a French Communist commando. But these criticisms were always directed to a specific person or event and never detracted from the journal's opinion of the Party as such. They were intended to correct the Party.

Even the anti-Semitic manifestations that marked the end of the Stalinist era in Russia and some of the popular democracies caused no serious breach between the existentialists and the French Communist Party. But *Ce Soir* published a fairly violent series of articles to which *L'Observateur* took exception. In *Le Figaro,* on March 17, 1953, François Mauriac called on Sartre to take a position and Sartre accepted. He was disturbed by Mauriac, who had started the polemic and called attention to Sartre's pronouncements in order to "declare war." "I hope for the rebirth of an independent Left working in close cooperation with the Communist Party," Sartre said. "What would independence mean if we began by denying ourselves the right to say what we believe to be true? . . . In a journal which claims to deal with contemporary problems we have the absolute duty to say what we think about matters we know something about." Sartre recalled that "even silence was a form of commitment." [12]

"I have no intention of trying to justify dialectically anti-Semitism," he added. But he would not adopt the tone of *Le Figaro* or the B.E.I.P.I. "I do not write, and Mr. Mauriac must know this, to be praised for editing a journal which did not protest the plight of the Jews. The problem and condition of the Jews in the popular democracies should not be a pretext for propaganda or a polemical joust. When I speak of this problem, obviously without attempting an impossible 'dialectical justification,' I will address myself to my friends on the Left, Communist or not, Jews or not, for the problem concerns them and for them only it is dramatic. Only they, and not Mr. Mauriac, have the right to interrogate me about what I think, and they are the only ones I should wish to interrogate about their thinking."

As a matter of fact, the journal published an article by Marcel Péju in May, 1953, on the Slansky affair. Well balanced and nuanced, it firmly and explicitly condemned anti-Semitism. The Party neither reacted nor criticized *Les Temps Modernes*. The Communists were pursuing an alliance with certain intellectuals, and it considered that unity was essential in the fight for peace. When it gave priority to a policy, all other considerations became secondary until that objective was attained. During the time of the cold war when allies were scarce and the struggle for peace was an absolute, the French Communist Party permitted criticism of their policy on other points provided they were supported in the struggle against war.

Thus the harmony between Sartre and communism increased. This was markedly noticeable in a series of articles he gave to *Libération* when he returned from a journey to the Soviet Union.[13] "I met a new breed of men there," Sartre reported. "It is impossible not to think of them as friends. Whatever road France takes must not contradict the way of Russia." The second article appeared under the title: "The freedom to criticize is total in Russia. Contact is as broad, open and easy as possible." Here Sartre affirmed that "from the beginning the Soviets trust man" and that in Russia man "is aware of the constant and harmonious progress of his own life as well as social life. Individual and collective interests coincide."

When Bedel asked Sartre if the "silenced" writers could still write, he answered, "Yes. Moreover, they have been advised to write new books to redeem themselves." Finally, Sartre stated that Russia wanted peace and prophesied that around 1960, and before 1965, if France continued to stagnate, the average standard of living in Russia would be from 30 to 40 percent higher than its own. "It is quite evident to everybody," he concluded, "that the only reasonable relationship is one of friendship."

Libération gave a good deal of publicity to this series of articles and Bedel noted that "Sartre's trip [to the Soviet Union] would undoubtedly mark a date in the history of relations between French intellectuals and that great country."

When Simone de Beauvoir's *The Mandarins* appeared, the Communist press chided her for portraying Communists who were "docile, somewhat Machiavellian and not very happy." But de Beauvoir insisted that her book was not hostile to Communists. The only interview she granted after she received the Prix Goncourt appeared in *L'Humanité-Dimanche*. She insisted that she was sympathetic to her Communist protagonists and had portrayed them as somewhat difficult in order to pose certain problems to the intelligentsia. J. F. Rolland readily admitted that if the Communists had been presented too sympathetically it would have weakened the political development of these *mandarins*. Thus they congratulated one another on their mutual understanding.

The political alliance that Sartre had established with the French Communist Party was real enough. Stalin's death, and the end of certain policies, facilitated the *rapprochement*. It is by no means certain that Sartre could have maintained this friendship had the tactics of the *blouses blanches* continued. He hoped for a renewal of the Communist movement and was convinced that one could only criticize fruitfully as an ally and not an enemy. In general political terms, his goal was first of all to affirm his solidarity with the Party (which alone gave him a possibility of criticizing positively) and then to combat anti-communism as strenuously as possible.[14] It is easy to see why Merleau-Ponty's "a-communism" was irreconcilable with such a position.

The political rupture between Sartre and Merleau-Ponty began in 1950; their friendship ended in 1953 when Merleau definitively took leave of *Les Temps Modernes*. After the deception he had suffered in 1950 he refused to discuss politics until 1955. His point of view had not changed; and he said that it was necessary to choose between the Revolution as action and as truth. In other words, Marxist truth failed because by incarnating itself in a regime it became an ideology like any other system. Revolutionary mediation between the proletariat and the Party never functioned.

Merleau-Ponty's *Les Aventures de la dialectique* was also published in 1955.[15] The book was to "mark out the path of experience from the point of view of political philosophy rather than politics itself." The meaning of history does not reveal itself clearly. In reality, it is more a question "of eliminating the non-meaning of history" than establishing its meaning; and this non-meaning is not easily eliminated. On the contrary, the Revolution has become institutionalized and is already outside of time, living in the future. It had thwarted its own meaning; a theory on the proletariat, which was its guarantee and motor force, was not clearly formulated. Consequently, it floundered in idealistic voluntarism. It tried to force reality and still proclaim its truth (which was no longer truth); it tried to give the impression that the fire still burned when merely ashes existed, as Sperber put it. And in the name of this extinguished fire, in a last effort despite themselves to warm men's hearts, it killed and excommunicated its traitors, those who no longer believed, those who proclaimed that the fire had gone out. "To be a revolutionary today is to accept a State we know little about or abandon ourselves to a History about which we know still less; nor can this be done without misery and tears. Is it therefore cheating to demand that the dice be checked?" [16] In his epilogue Merleau-Ponty called upon men "to bear their freedom, not to exchange it at a loss, for it is not only theirs, their secret, their pleasure, their salvation, but of interest to all men."

In a word, Merleau-Ponty refused to grant a new reprieve to the Marxist dialectic. His future analyses would be methodologically more like those of Max Weber than Marx. He had lost faith in the dialectic. Out of fear of voluntarist transcendence—and the illusory and bloody character this kind of transcendence easily takes on—he finally repudiated all forms of transcendence and synthesis.

Sartre, on the other hand, maintained that there is always a transcendence. The best form of synthesis does not necessarily take place, but it exists nonetheless. For Merleau-Ponty, contradiction is not a human conflict; it is a characteristic of abstract being. The dialectic dissolves in pluralism. Contradictions reflect one another, as though through so many mirrors, in a circular reciprocity that denies history.

This was a fundamental theoretical and political debate. But it would not have come to the public's attention had Merleau-Ponty not challenged Sartre in the fifth chapter of his book, "Sartre and Ultra-Bolshevism." The attack was a serious one. Sartre saw himself accused of maintaining the insularity of consciences, of abolishing the dialectic (Marxist or other) without duly considering its merits, of maintaining a voluntarism which was merely an attempt to mask reality. Merleau-Ponty attacked progressivism mercilessly for "its dreamy gentleness, its incurable stubbornness, its velvet-gloved violence." Simone de Beauvoir responded in *Les Temps Modernes*. She accused him of deliberately lying about Sartre's thought, of drawing his anti-Communist arguments from the columns of *L'Aurore*, of taking the side of the bourgeoisie, and of being an unfortunate victim of the traditional idealism that has always plagued French intellectuals. This was the only public outburst between Merleau-Ponty and *Les Temps Modernes*. Each tried to forget it as soon as possible.

Notes

1 · Sartre, J.-P., "Merleau-Ponty," *Situations,* tr. Benita Eisler (New York, Braziller, 1965), pp. 88–89. Reprinted with permission. English translation copyright © 1965 by George Braziller, Inc.

2 · *Ibid.,* p. 352.

3 · The Sartre-Camus quarrel received much more publicity than Sartre wanted or than it deserved. It was, moreover, quite evident since the Liberation that the two writers were very dissimilar and that Camus' "stubborn humanism, narrow and pure, austere and sensual" (see Sartre's "Reply to Albert Camus," *Situations, ibid.,* p. 110) was not of a nature to please Sartre. There were profound political and philosophical differences between the moralist and the "engaged" writer. It seems that Sartre was sparing in his criticism first of all out of friendship for Camus and, secondly, for fear that their common political enemies would benefit by the quarrel. The pages of *Les Temps Modernes* were still open to Camus in August, 1951, when he published an article on "Nietzsche and Nihilism." Camus' vain and brittle rejoinder to Francis Jeanson's review of *The Rebel* destroyed this coexistence. From the public point of view, the sequence of events was as follows: 1. Francis Jeanson, "Albert Camus ou l'âme révoltée (review of *The Rebel*), *Les Temps Modernes,* No. 79, June, 1952, pp. 2077–90. 2. Albert Camus, "Lettre au directeur des *Temps Modernes,*" *Les Temps Modernes,* No. 82, August, 1952, pp. 317–33. 3. J.-P. Sartre "Réponse à Albert Camus," *Les Temps Modernes,* No. 82, August, 1952, pp. 334–53. 4. Francis Jeanson, "Pour tout vous dire," *Les Temps Modernes,* No. 82, August, 1952, pp. 354–83. See the Appendix, pp. 175ff., for a full account of the quarrel.

4 · Sartre, J.-P., "Reply to Albert Camus," *Situations, op. cit.,* p. 78. The following citations are from the same source: pp. 77, 98, 100 and 103.

5 · Sartre, J.-P., "Les Communistes et la paix (III)," *Les Temps Modernes, op. cit.,* p. 1735. The following nine citations of Sartre are from the same source, pp. 1735-74.

6 · This analysis of French society in terms of Malthusianism can

be validly applied to the pre-1939 period. But it is more difficult to apply Malthusianism to French capitalism after 1945.
We can understand how Sartre was able to do so if we recall
that the years 1951–53 were years of stagnation. He could
quite naturally have thought that affairs were reverting to a
prewar state and that the period of economic reconstruction
had been merely an interlude. With respect to his thinking at
this time, Sartre told me in 1963 that his article ceased to be
exact as soon as he finished writing it. What seemed to him to
characterize French society after the war was the conflict between an expanding capitalism and reactionary elements in the
class structure. At the present time, he said, neo-capitalism replaced Malthusianism.

7 · Sartre, J.-P., "Les Communistes et la paix (III)," *Les Temps
Modernes, op cit.*, p. 1773 and p. 1818.

8 · Claude Lefort, an old collaborator on *Les Temps Modernes,*
had been a Trotskyite.

9 · Sartre, J.-P., "Réponse à Lefort," *Les Temps Modernes, op.
cit.*, p. 1573.

10 · During an interview in 1965.

11 · Sartre, J.-P., "Les Communistes et la paix (II)," *Les Temps
Modernes, op. cit.*, p. 761.

12 · Sartre, J.-P., "Réponse à M. Mauriac," *L'Observateur*, March
19, 1953.

13 · "Les Impressions de Jean-Paul Sartre sur son voyage en
U.R.S.S.," collected by Jean Bedel in *Libération*, July 20, 1954.

14 · This is the meaning of a play like *Nekrassov*. Here Sartre
tried to show the abjection and deceit of the daily press in
its battle against Russia and the French Communist Party. The
violent satire is directed not only against the technicians of
anti-communism but also against those Leftists who hoped that
"true socialism" would rise out of the ashes of the Soviet Republic.

15 · Merleau-Ponty, M., *Les Aventures de la dialectique* (Paris,
Gallimard, 1955)

16 · *Ibid.*, p. 313.

Chapter

7

THE HENRI MARTIN AFFAIR AND
THE HUNGARIAN REVOLUTION

WHEREAS Merleau-Ponty was thinking about preserving options for later use (the time came soon enough with the Mollet government and Gaullism), Sartre and *Les Temps Modernes* committed their freedom to action in the here and now. Up to 1957 the journal carried on an intense effort in political education.

Sartre undertook a study of Communist politics, outlined a framework of possible action and defined himself in relation to political realities because he wanted to influence daily events and take an active part in political life.

He did so primarily by fighting against the war in Indochina. He did everything he could to support the Communist Party's efforts to free Henri Martin, a soldier who had been imprisoned for distributing literature against the war. Martin was released as a result of popular pressure. To cut short a controversy that was becoming politically dangerous, the government gave in. Sartre published *L'Af-*

faire Henri Martin,[1] in which he collected the documents and articles relevant to the affair both to denounce the war in Indochina and the errors of the French government.

Les Temps Modernes also published many articles and various personal views on the war. It called insistently for negotiations with Ho Chi Minh; the August–September, 1953, issue was devoted to Vietnam. Then came Dien-Bien-Phu. A May, 1954, editorial clarifying the antiwar position read in part: "In vain have we tried to trick history and escape the evidence; the war is lost. When an occupation army is defeated by the national Resistance, when professional soldiers are routed by the people's army, when an anachronistic conflict ends in catastrophe, the ending is healthy and the defeat is just. One can die bravely; but one dies in vain."

This was also the era of McCarthyism. *Les Temps Modernes* took an adamant position: It became violently anti-American. Not only did the journal defend the Rosenbergs—as did many others—but it questioned the entire American system. After the Rosenbergs' execution, Sartre exploded: "The Rosenbergs are dead and life goes on. That is what you wanted, isn't it? . . . It was a legal lynching which covers whole nations with blood and clearly denounces once and for all the failure of the Atlantic Pact and your incapacity to assume leadership of the Western world.

". . . The Rosenberg affair is our affair; it is the affair of the whole world. . . . Everyone told you: 'Beware, you judge yourselves by judging them; it is a matter of deciding whether you are going to be men or animals. . . . And since we have become your allies, what happened to the Rosenbergs might well presage what will happen to us. You who pretend to be masters of the world had the opportunity to prove that you were first of all masters of yourselves. But you succumbed to criminal folly, and this same madness could in the future throw us all indiscriminately into a war of extermination.

". . . Only yesterday all of Europe—her people, her religious ministers and her heads of state—asked your president to make the simplest and most human of gestures. We didn't ask for your dollars or your weapons or your soldiers; no, we merely asked that two innocent lives be spared. . . . Did you understand the meaning of this extraordinary truce? Class conflicts, old grudges, everything was set aside; the Rosenbergs had effected the unity of Europe. One word from you and you, too, would have benefited by this unity. All of Europe would have thanked you. And you answered: 'To hell with Europe.' Very well. But don't ever again talk to us about alliance.

"We, your allies? Come now. Today our governments are your servants. Tomorrow our people will be your victims. It is as simple as that. . . . Do you think we are going to die for McCarthy? Sacrifice everything to give him a European army? Do you believe we want to defend McCarthy's civilization? McCarthy's freedom? McCarthy's justice? That we would turn Europe into a battlefield so this bloody fool can burn our books? And murder the innocent and imprison the judges who defend them? Do not be deceived: we will *never* give the leadership of the Western world to the murderers of the Rosenbergs."

And Sartre, who did not hesitate to talk about American fascism, wrote in *Libération* in June, 1953, "Meanwhile, do not be surprised if we shout from one end of Europe to the other: 'Beware, America has the rabies. Let us cut the bonds that bind us to her; otherwise we will in our turn be bitten and infected.' "

The editorial for July, 1953, was also devoted to the execution of the Rosenbergs. It took up the same themes and denounced the apathy of the American masses. The Dreyfus affair had divided France, but Dreyfus had been pardoned. How many Americans protested the execution of two innocent people? America was afraid—it was afraid of socialism and its own bomb. The editorial denounced the American secret police, spoke of totalitarianism and expressed anger at "economic assassination." The intervention of the marines against the democratic regime of Arbenz, in Guatemala, lent force to these criticisms.

But the chief concern of *Les Temps Modernes* from 1954 on was Algeria. Early in 1953 Daniel Guérin had written in the journal about the North African problem. Colonization had already been radically condemned, and the journal had already stated that "the North African drama was, in the final analysis, somewhat similar to the drama of the French Left." Claude Bourdet wrote in the journal about the problems of Morocco. In November, 1953, Habib Bourguiba wrote an article in which he criticized sharply Mendès-France for his Algerian policy. Then, in October, 1955, an editorial on Algeria was entitled: "Refusal of Obedience." "In North Africa today, France must rule by terror or be wiped out." The war had become serious and the government gave the Algerian people only one alternative—to fight. Collective repressions, racism, torture, rigged elections, banned papers and democratic parties —this was France's image in Algeria. Therefore, the editorial concluded, "We say no to this war." The following issue dealt with the war and carried the general title: "Algeria Is Not France." It explicitly called for negotiation and independence. There were frequent reports on the war in the journal. The vote of full powers to Guy Mollet was criticized. On January 27, 1956, the Committee of Intellectuals for Action against the continuation of the war in North Africa held a meeting in the Salle Wagram, where Jean-Paul Sartre, one of the members of the committee, said, "The desired reforms will come in their time. The Algerian people will bring them about. The only thing that we can and should do—and it is essential today that we do—is to fight at their side in order to deliver *both* Algeria and France from colonial tyranny."

Claude Bourdet's arrest by the Mollet government provoked *T.M.* violently. The June, 1956, editorial accused Mollet of reviving witch hunts. The same issue published an article by Mostefa Lacheraf.

But the fight against colonial wars and McCarthyism was only a "negative moment"; it was not enough to proclaim one's attachment to the Party and reject colonial wars; one had to propose the political means for change. Such change, in the opinion of *Les Temps Modernes*, could be brought about by a Popular Front. In this matter the journal did not identify with the so-called "New Left." Far from it. For a start, it opposed the attitudes expressed by *L'Express*, particularly its position on the Algerian war.

The supporters of Pierre Mendès-France, on the other hand, condemned the policies of *Les Temps Modernes*, which they considered to be based on false premises. "As a matter of principle, a Left that seeks to define itself in relation to the Communist Party will be doomed to equivocation and failure," wrote Alain Gourdon in *Le Jacobin*. "To identify the working class with the Communist Party and refuse to cut oneself off from the one in order not to betray the other was the false premise of their [the existentialists'] action. Starting off with an inferiority complex, they mingled camaraderie, aversions and impassioned spite, and ended with an ambiguous morality that only won them the scorn of those they have long sought as allies." The article concluded bitterly: "Fascinated by the boa, they consoled themselves with the knowledge that they were indigestible." [2]

The existentialists of *Les Temps Modernes* were as immoderate in their rejoinder. When J.-F. Rolland remarked to Simone de Beauvoir that many of the *mandarins* now believed in Mendès-France, she answered: "That could only be because of bad faith or a misunderstanding. One would have to be very naïve indeed to think that a Leftist political program could be carried out with a majority from the Right. The criminal attitude of the government before the North African problems, its obstinancy in rearming Germany, its economic 'program' that scarcely dissimulates procrastination under promised reforms, all of this will eventually open people's eyes and reveal the truth of what can only be called Mendès-France's mystification." [3]

Les Temps Modernes also cast a cool eye on *France-Observateur*. Martinet, Sartre pointed out, "at first said no to Stalinist communism freely, but weakened by humiliations and insults, he lost the freedom to say yes." [4]

While there was still some hope for the Left during Mendès-France's government, *Les Temps Modernes* had defined what seemed to them a realizable and realistic program. This was remarkable in that it was the first time the French existentialists had actually defined a political program—not merely a number of reforms but the concrete means of carrying them out as well. The total picture was for the first time thought out in terms of the state, political strength and immediate possibilities.

The journal approved of the termination of the war in Indochina, the Carthage agreements and the rejection of the C.E.D., while it criticized the government's policy in Algeria and the rearmament of Germany. ("Courage for the Left does not mean obliterating the policies of the Right.") If Mendès-France's program was to be effective there would have to be a coalition of the Popular Front. It was important that the Communists, without self-contradiction, be able to support Mendès-France's government (although their support was not accepted).

"In a word, Mendès-France's actions really implied the broad outline of a policy that needed only its author's will to crystallize. That policy is easily defined. Domestically, it should accept Communist support without needless moral torments, and profiting by public opinion on the German problem, regroup the Popular Front to bring about practical programs of economic and social reforms and negotiations with the East. In Vietnam it should quickly liquidate the Buddhist fanatics and inaugurate a broad-based and loyal collaboration with the democratic republic while waiting for its electoral victory. In Algeria and Morocco it should, as it did in Tunisia, accede to nationalist demands. In foreign policy, finally resigning itself to the uselessness of the Atlantic Alliance and refusing to lend support to German rearmament, it should begin frank negotiations with the Soviet Union on common European questions to the eventual end of general conference." [5]

Les Temps Modernes did not consider this policy idealistic. It would be a false realism to accept the status quo.

This program at least held out hope for some changes. "All the elements of this new policy were of a piece." In Parliament the majority should solicit the collaboration of "the Communists, half of the Socialists and the U.D.S.R., the majority of Radicals and the R.P.F. In foreign affairs, it should play members of the Labour Party against the Conservatives and, within the Labour Party, Bevan against Atlee, in Germany the Social Democrats against the Christian Socialists—in a word, the future against the past." [6]

The problem was not to prove that such a policy was realizable. What was important was that the editors of *Les Temps Modernes* could demonstrate that reforms were possible. Their principal preoccupation was the problem of the unity of the Left. The journal's double issue on "The Left" in 1955 must be understood in this perspective. They set out to define this political notion, to set specific tasks for it that would forge its unity. The chapter headings were significant: "Definitions," "History," "Tasks." The contributors were also of considerable importance. In addition to Simone de Beauvoir, they included such former Communists as Dyonis Mascolo, representatives of the "New Left" (Claude Bourdet, Gilles Martinet), Trotskyites (Pierre Naville), members of the independent Left (Maurice Duverger, Georges E. Lavau, Alfred Sauvy, René Dumont) and delegates from the Communist Party (Victor Leduc and Jean Desanti).

The conclusion, signed "Temps Modernes," was entitled: "Toward a Popular Front." It stated that "the Left exists in part to protest against the Right." It did not try to minimize differences but simply expressed the hope that the Left would rally to a common task as they had to end the war in Indochina. But since "the Communist Party could make no concessions short of suppressing itself," the principal challenge consisted in fighting against anti-communism.

Les Temps Modernes had been pushing this for a number of years and would continue to do so until November, 1956. At that time the Hungarian Revolution exploded like a thunderclap in Western intellectual circles. For *Les Temps Modernes*, it was truly the end of an era.

In 1961 Sartre declared: "Budapest was a case of aggression and war. It was a socialist nation which took the initiative in this intervention and deliberately went contrary to the very structures and principles of socialism." By this time everything could be questioned. The reactions were extremely lively.

On November 9, 1956, Sartre published an article in *L'Express*. He explained the intervention and proclaimed that he was aware of the threat of "a return to reaction." "But to explain is not to excuse. From every point of view, the intervention was a crime. It is an abject lie to pretend that the workers are fighting side by side with the Soviet troops." "The Red Army opened fire on an entire nation." Sartre denounced "twelve years of terror and stupidity." "What the Hungarian people teach us with their blood is the complete failure of socialism as a merchandise imported from Russia." Sartre thought that the plight of the Left in France was hopeless. One could no longer choose between those who approved the Soviet intervention and the S.F.I.O. which concealed the tortures in Algeria. Sartre said unequivocally that he was breaking with the French Communist Party.

Maurice Merleau-Ponty also spoke out. "The Hungarian Communists' insurrection means that Stalinism has reached to the socialist essence of the regime." "The homage we owe the Hungarians is to understand their sacrifice and explain it for all to hear so that it may not have been in vain." [7]

These statements provoked considerable consternation. To Sartre, who had praised the courage of the Hungarian Union of Writers, Roger Garaudy replied by saying that the Hungarian writers "were apprentice sorcerers, blinded like him [Sartre] by their proud individualism." Thirty-five Soviet writers publicly disapproved the French writers' protest against the Soviet intervention which Sartre had signed,[8] and the Frenchmen, in turn, answered back in *France-Observateur*.

Finally, on December 1 and 2, in the presence of Laurent Casanova, Sartre and other non-Communists succeeded in having the National Council of the Peace Movement pass a resolution calling for the withdrawal of Soviet troops.

Les Temps Modernes continued its analysis in the November–January issue, the only triple number of its history, entitled "The Revolt of Hungary." A long article by Sartre preceded pieces by Hungarian writers. In his article Sartre tried to shed some light on the problems that had been raised suddenly by the Hungarian situation.[9] He noted first that only those who came out against the tortures and massacres in Algeria, the Suez affair and all other armed interventions had the right to protest. He then affirmed his total opposition to Stalinist terrorism and its aftermath, principally the Soviet intervention in Hungary. But while he denounced the Communist police state, imprisonments and the stupid exportation of a Soviet socialism that ignored the economic and social conditions of the popular democracies, he continued to maintain that the bureaucracy, while overpaid, was not essentially an exploiting class and that the Soviet Union had not colonized its satellites. The most serious problem both he and the journal confronted was what kind of relationship they should establish with the French Communists. To protest the policies of Russia would be an abstract matter if they did not come to terms with the Party in their own country. Sartre did not succumb to anti-Communist hysteria, but he wrote that the French Communist Party had *cut itself off from the masses* and its proposal for a common front with other Leftist parties made unity impossible. The French Communist Party was totally incompetent, totally impotent. During the Suez crisis it hadn't accomplished half what the Labour Party in England had. The Party was "frozen"; it had never de-Stalinized. "The structure of the Party is in flagrant contradiction to its policies; consequently, the latter necessarily remain inoperative and unrealistic." "Consider this monstrous Party which blocks and freezes five million voices, demobilizes the working class, abandons the interests of the masses for parliamentary maneuvers, lightly denounces Algeria in order to threaten the socialists, quite in vain, but at the same time does not hesitate to rationalize its contempt with stupid declarations about the situation in Hungary."

"For our part," Sartre concluded, "we have engaged in dialogue with the Communists for twelve years. At first fiercely and then in friendship. But our aim has always been the same: to collaborate as much as possible in establishing unity among leftist groups which *alone* can save our country. Today we return to the opposition for the simple reason that there is no other alternative. Alliance with the

Communist Party as it is and intends to remain can have no other effect than compromising the last chances for a common front." [10]

How did Sartre see the role of *Les Temps Modernes?* At the end of the article he stated: "With our intellectual resources and readership, we will try to de-Stalinize the French Communist Party." Wasn't this goal defined by Sartre the very same which Merleau-Ponty assigned the Left at the end of his November, 1956, article? "A Leftist is a man who desires the success of de-Stalinization, a de-Stalinization which is unchecked, consequential and extends beyond the frontiers of communism to the whole Left that communism has 'frozen.' " [11]

The two paths of French existentialism rapidly crossed at this time.

Notes

1 · *L'Affaire Henri Martin*, commentary by Jean-Paul Sartre, texts by Hervé Bazin, J.-M. Domenach, F. Jeanson, J. Madaule, R. Pinto, Jacques Prevert, Vercors, etc. (Paris, Gallimard, 1953).

2 · This striking image was not original with Gourdon; nor was it drawn from the radical tradition. It was in fact plagiarized from something Sartre himself wrote in 1950 and which Gourdon must have forgotten. "I cannot laugh at the nausea of the Communist boa constrictor, unable either to keep down or vomit up the enormous Picasso. In the C.P.'s indigestion, I see the symptoms of an infection which contaminates our entire era." See Sartre, J.-P., "The Artist and His Conscience," *Situations*, tr. Benita Eisler (New York, Braziller, 1965), p. 206.

3 · Interview with Simone de Beauvoir in *L'Humanité-Dimanche*, December 19, 1954.

4 · Sartre, J.-P., "Réponse à Pierre Naville," *Les Temps Modernes*, No. 123, March–April, 1956, p. 1525. The same article reproached the New Left with using methods in political discussion worthy of *Le Figaro*.

5 · *Ibid.*, p. 964. See Péju, M., "Pierre Mendès-France ou les ambiguités," *Les Temps Modernes*, No. 109, January–February, 1955, p. 964.

6 · *Ibid.*

7 · Merleau-Ponty, M., "On De-Stalinization," *Signs*, tr. Richard McCleary (Evanston, Illinois, Northwestern University Press, 1964), pp. 293–94.

8 · The petition, signed by Sartre, Claude Roy, Roger Vailland, Jacques Madaule, Vercors, etc., read as follows: "Never having had inimical feelings toward the U.S.S.R., we think that today we have the right to protest against the use of cannons and tanks to put down the revolt of the Hungarian people."

9 · Sartre, J.-P., "Le Fantôme de Staline," *Les Temps Modernes*, Nos. 129–131, November, 1956–January, 1957, pp. 577–696.

10 · Francis Jeanson, who had published *Algérie hors la loi* in 1955, disapproved of this attitude. Deeply concerned by the Al-

gerian problem, he devoted most of his time to fighting against the war. For different reasons he had not collaborated on *Les Temps Modernes* for several years, but his name remained on the masthead as manager. When Sartre learned that Jeanson was privately criticizing his views on Hungary, he removed his name from the journal. This was the only outward sign of a dispute that was to last for several years.

11 · Merleau-Ponty, M., "On De-Stalinization," *Signs, op. cit.,* p. 308.

Part III

FOR A DISRESPECTFUL LEFT

1956 – 1965

Chapter

8

REDISCOVERING DEMOCRACY

By 1957 THE BREAK with the French Communists was complete.[1] And as well with the S.F.I.O. An article on Guy Mollet bore the heading: "He Disgraces the Name of Socialism." *Les Temps Modernes* opposed the Algerian war absolutely. Describing French methods of "pacification," Sartre wrote in May, 1957: "That is the evidence, that is the horror, and it is ours. We cannot behold it without desiring to crush it."

At this dramatic time of the Hungarian repression, the Algerian war and the confiscation of newspapers,[2] the editors of *Les Temps Modernes* cried out: "We must cry out, it is necessary to howl like a man who has been stabbed, if only because one cannot tolerate the pain in silence."

Les Temps Modernes followed the Hungarian situation very closely, first because *T.M.* must defend the rights of man, but also because the editors believed that *rapprochement* between the intellectual Left and Russia was totally dependent on the real situation in Hungary, and Sartre added that they would stick by their position as long as Budapest was the object of repression and oppression. Tibor Meray was invited to explain the events of 1956 in the journal, and *Les Temps Modernes* also called for the freedom of Tibor Dery.

But in spite of everything the Algerian problem was becoming increasingly critical, and the editors continued to publish numerous testimonies. When the Bourgès-Maunoury ministry collapsed, the journal once against asked the Socialists to stop allying themselves with the Right and at last propose a progressive policy for Algeria. In December, 1957, Sartre testified at Ben Saddok's trial, and toward the end of January, 1958, Simone de Beauvoir intervened on behalf of Jacqueline Guerroudj.

In 1957 *Les Temps Modernes* was seized four times in Algeria. After Raffaello Uboldi's article had appeared in November, it was seized for the first time in France. The journal retorted that the government had only one answer to the accumulated testimony, accusations and facts—seizure. As for Robert Lacoste, he was considered "a Socialist gone mad."

When Henri Alleg published *La Question*, in which he described how he had been tortured by the French army, this group of French existentialists multiplied their intercessions. The March, 1958, issue of *Les Temps Modernes* carried several articles on Algeria. Sartre wrote an article on Henri Alleg's book, and the edition of *L'Express* in which it appeared was seized. In his article Sartre had tried to show that torture was not an accident in the kind of war that was being waged but an essential part of it. "To end these foul and dismal cruelties we have but one means: begin negotiations and make peace."

But at this time Sartre did not seem to have any specific suggestions for ending the war. *Les Temps Modernes* appealed to the intellectuals and tried to stir up public opinion. They joined their efforts with other groups in order to be heard. Sartre participated in a press conference on "The Violation of Human Rights in Algeria" with Laurent Schwartz, François Mauriac, the president of the French bar (Thorp), General Billotte and Mrs. Henri Alleg.

There were no strict alliances. *Les Temps Modernes* sided unconditionally with the adversaries of the war but could not join ranks with the Communist Party as they had done during the Henri Martin affair and the Indochinese war.

On what ideological basis could the campaign be waged? Their answer was a renewed socialism. However serious their break with the Communist Party and the Soviet Union, the French existentialists still held that the hope of mankind could best be safeguarded by a movement within the Party itself.

If the years 1954–56 were the "Algerian period" of *Les Temps Modernes,* the years 1957–58 were its "Polish period." The journal endeavored to inform itself on Polish communism. The February–March, 1957, issue, dedicated to this subject, contained numerous poems, articles and reports that had appeared in Polish newspapers and journals between 1954 and 1957. A prefatory note indicated the spirit with which Polish communism was welcomed: "We finally see here what should be, what can be today and will be tomorrow—a communism liberated from Stalinism." In Poland, "the Party itself, despite a certain opposition from within, took over the leadership of the democratic movement." "The aberrations, mystifications and nightmares of Stalinism are denounced here by those who were its victims and its instruments as well. Still they deny nothing of what they have done. They are responsible for all. They were mistaken, but only because they sought the truth. . . . In Poland today the revolution is thawing. 'We have crossed the Rubicon. It is spring in October,' said Radio Warsaw."

During 1957 the Polish Communists took the initiative in contacting Sartre. In the winter of that year he published "Existentialism and Marxism" in the Polish journal, *Tworcose*.[3] Marcel Péju went to Poland to cement relationships. *Les Temps Modernes* published articles and documents on Poland over a number of months and their editorial policy was always pro-Gomulka.

It is paradoxical that during these years when there was philosophical agreement with the methods of Marxism and immense sympathy for the popular democracies, when there was no disagreement on a number of basic points between the Party and *Les Temps Modernes*, contact had been broken off with the French Communist Party. No political accord seemed possible with it. In practice it represented the opposite of the 1952–54 problem, when the two groups were in political agreement but at loggerheads philosophically.

Added to the double-pronged campaign for peace in Algeria and the establishment of democracy within communism, a third issue was added: the cause against Gaullism. In May, 1958, *Les Temps Modernes* proclaimed its absolute opposition to General de Gaulle, "the general of pronunciamentos who, despite his aspirations for 'grandeur,' is reducing France to the rank of a South American dictatorship of the last century."

De Gaulle was the "geometrical point of all our impotence and all our contradictions. . . . The solitude of this man imprisoned in his grandeur disqualifies him from becoming the leader of a Republican state or, what amounts to the same thing, incapacitates any state he would head from remaining a Republic." [4] In July, the journal joined the Communists in appealing to the opposition. It urged the minority of the S.F.I.O. to break away, "for this would be the first sign of life for a new Left and the means by which the Communist Party could finally undergo a renewal without fear of weakening itself. This new Left is the only hope of one day triumphing over the common enemy."

Simone de Beauvoir recalls in *Force of Circumstance* how she participated in demonstrations for the defense of the Republic on May 30 and September 4, 1958, joined anti-fascist committees, and took part in anti-Gaullist demonstrations during the summer of 1958.

Jean-Paul Sartre objected fiercely to de Gaulle's referendum of September 28, 1958. He denounced it in *L'Express* as an insult to the popular sovereignty: "We have only one answer to this truncated plebiscite: No. Let us not fall into the ultimate trap. Let us not be 'the spirit that always denies.' We have been deliberately forced to a pure and simple refusal; let us reorganize and give meaning to this refusal. Let our No to the monarchy signify the 'Constituent Assembly.' " [5] (This was one of the basic demands of the Communists.)

Sartre continued to denounce the bill. Four pages in a later issue of *L'Express* were devoted to an article of his which carried the give-away title: "Frogs Who Demand a King." The article was instructive and the argument simple. It aimed explicitly at shaking up "perfectly honest and radically democratic voters" who might vote Yes.

"Yes is a dream," said Sartre; "No is an awakening. It is time to decide whether we want to wake up or go to sleep." [6]

For those who chose to wake up, *Les Temps Modernes* proposed to reorganize the Left, to make it over. From a somewhat different point of view Merleau-Ponty was suggesting the same thing. His anti-Gaullism was as violent as that of *Les Temps Modernes*; in his mind "General de Gaulle's appearance . . . is also the sequel to and so to speak the masterpiece of Molletism." He went so far as to add: "I am not sure that this might not be the end." Like Sartre, he feared the General's paternalism and the abdication of the French people, who owed General de Gaulle "something other and better than devotion; we owe him our opinion. He is too young to be our father and we are too old to act like children." [7]

But Merleau-Ponty thought that "the real questions could be asked only aside from both the Right and the Communists, with the hope that they as well as the country would end by taking a real interest in them." However, to oppose Gaullism effectively and assure a liberal policy overseas, Merleau-Ponty thought there was no way other than to rely on those who voted Communist and thereby helped the Party's renewal, for otherwise "there will not be any democracy in France." But "it is not of restoring the Republic, above all the Republic we have had for the past two years, that we need think. We must think of re-creating it free of its rituals and obsessions, in the light of day." Because the old machinery of the S.F.I.O. and the Communist Party was incapable of doing this, Merleau-Ponty supported Pierre Mendès-France and his Committee for Democratic Action (C.A.D.). He agreed anyhow with the former President's socialist leanings, and was, at the end of 1958, a member of the U.F.D. along with another philosopher who is sometimes considered an existentialist, Jean Hyppolite, the director of the École Normale Supérieure. In order to wage an anti-Gaullist campaign from the non-Communist Left, the U.F.D. reorganized the former minorities of the S.F.I.O. (the P.S.A.), the C.A.D., the U.G.S. and the Mitterand wing of the U.D.S.R.

In these times of crisis, Merleau-Ponty and Sartre fought the same battle in different ways. But Merleau-Ponty's methods were more ad hoc, Sartre's more radical. On the level of political philosophy they were worlds apart.[8]

Notes

1 · Sartre, however, did not resign from the C.N.E. or the Peace Movement. He even kept up personal contacts with the Soviet intellectuals and especially Ilya Ehrenburg. *The Respectful Prostitute* played in Moscow in 1957.

2 · *France-Observateur*, for example, was seized twice between April 11 and May 2, 1957. *Les Temps Modernes*, June, 1957, reprinted the articles that were the cause of the confiscation.

3 · This was later reprinted as *Search for a Method*, tr. Hazel Barnes (New York, Knopf, 1963). Here Sartre defines Marxism as the culture of our time but defends the philosophy of existentialism in the absence of a better one provided by Marxism. But his explicit aim is to hasten the dissolution of existentialism in the broader movement of an "unfrozen" Marxism. It is therefore important to note that Sartre no longer approves of the revolution and at the same time is trying to create a new revolutionary philosophy. He considers himself a participant in the construction of Marxism with the Communists and asserts unequivocally that Marxism is the indispensable framework which alone can do justice to the history of our era.

4 · Sartre, J.-P., "Le Prétendant," *L'Express*, May 22, 1958.

5 · The first article, "La Constitution du mépris," was published in *L'Express*, September 11, 1958.

6 · *L'Express*, September 25, 1958.

7 · Merleau-Ponty, M., "On May 13, 1958," *Signs*, tr. Richard McCleary (Evanston, Illinois, Northwestern University Press, 1964), p. 337. In the beginning of this article Merleau-Ponty points out that Guy Mollet is "a traitor to his socialism, then to the defense of the Republic" (p. 337).

8 · On the philosophical plane Merleau-Ponty affirmed the possibility of a third way between neo-capitalism and the spread of the Russian dictatorship. See the debate on "L'Avenir du socialisme," over which he presided; reprinted in *Cahiers de la République*, No. XXII, November–December, 1959, especially pp. 31, 32, 35 and 42.

Chapter

9

THE F.L.N. AND PEACE

Les Temps Modernes continued to denounce the pacification of Algeria and oppose the war throughout 1960. It appealed for negotiation, printed testimonies on the Algerian situation and offered analyses. But the editors noted that public reaction "was limited to certain circles that were always the same; an anesthetized public opinion followed scandal with extraordinary indifference."

It was Sartre's position that because of the Left's default they had to take a radical position. Such a "radical position" had been taken in 1957 by Francis Jeanson, a former collaborator on *Les Temps Modernes*. Profoundly impassioned by Algeria, Jeanson had in 1955 published a book[1] in which he had openly sided with the Algerian nationalists. He was deeply disturbed by the isolation he found himself in after the book came out, and wanting to organize a real solidarity with the Algerians, he undertook in 1957 to found a network of support for the F.L.N.

Sartre had, since that time, renewed contact with Jeanson and approved his action.[2] On February 23, 1960, the network was discovered by the police and several of its members were arrested.

When this became known there was a scandal and *Les Temps Modernes* openly expressed its agreement with Francis Jeanson. Thus from February, 1960, on, Jeanson, Péju, Sartre and others attempted to define a political theory that would justify their position.

"Our point of departure is the impotence of the Left."[3] Jeanson blamed the Communist Party for its lack of interest in colonial problems and for its failure to intervene on behalf of the prisoners in Algeria with the same enthusiasm it had for Henri Martin. He reproached the whole Left for having stood by awaiting the de-Stalinization of the Communist Party and the advent to power of Pierre Mendès-France without doing anything, on the pretext that public opinion was not mature. Sartre also referred to this impotence: "We have cried out, protested, signed, countersigned; we have, according to our accustomed way of thinking, declared: 'This is inadmissible' or 'The proletariat will not admit. . . .' And finally we reached the end of our energy and accepted everything. . . . From default to default we learned one thing: our essential impotence."[4]

Jeanson and Sartre defined the politics of the Right and its humanism which was the result of this impotence: "It was merely a deceptive ideology, the exquisite justification of pillage."[5] In this world of absolute violence in which, as Jeanson said, abstention favors "the side of the oppressors" and the Left betrays, they hoped to salvage what they could of Franco-Algerian friendship, and taking up arms on the side of the Algerians, lead the people back to their duty by stirring up public opinion. For, Sartre said, "all is lost unless we understand that we are at war and that objectively we belong to one or another of the camps." Jeanson could not speak of unjust war without admitting the justice of the cause of the F.L.N. It was impossible to oppose fascism and colonialism without joining forces with their most resolute adversaries, the Algerians. Even so to oppose fascism and colonialism with nationalism was, Jeanson thought, an error. National community, he explained, did not in fact exist and only fascists and "genuine internationalists" were honest in their opposing attempts to reform this community to their own advantage. He called, therefore, for participation in the combat to bring about the triumph of internationalism over nationalism.

Since sides had to be chosen and adhered to, and since any position taken amounted to acceptance of violence, whether voluntary or implicit, one should opt for the violence of the F.L.N. and fight on its side; the young must be encouraged to totally reject the war; therefore insubordination and desertion were to be supported.

But only an avant-garde could act as such a detonator and Jeanson had always maintained that such action "would make sense only in dialectical perspective, as a complement to official political action." [6] The members of the network counted at the very least on the positive neutralism of Leftist leaders and newspaper editors.

This did not turn out to be so. In February and March of 1960, the Leftist press published numerous condemnatory articles that were both categorical and severe. Apart from *Les Temps Modernes* no important journal, party or group backed the network. There was an open split between the members of the network and their allies, and

the rest of those opposed to the war. This rift was accentu-
ated when Jeanson and *Les Temps Modernes* pointed out
that many articles at this time were merely "answers
to. . . ." [7]

The tone of the debate was far from friendly. The
press called Jeanson's initiative traitorous at worst and at
best individualistic. Jeanson called Domenach "a stolid
spirit" and said his tone was an old man's, and warned that
J.-J. Servan-Schreiber risked "throwing the baby out with
the bath water," and that Jean Daniel understood Gaullism
only too well.

The allies of the network accused their accusers of be-
longing to the "respectable Left." In the April–May, 1960,
issue of *Les Temps Modernes* Marcel Péju accused the ad-
ministrations of the parties, organizations and journals of
being taken by surprise by such "unforeseen initiatives,"
and by "the only concrete action that the Left had taken
since the Resistance." "They read their own failure in the
'Jeanson network.'" Their own impotence—which *Les
Temps Modernes* had referred to so often since 1956—was
the cause of all defeats. There was a failure of leadership and
Les Temps Modernes discerned a renewal movement among
the young. That is why they chose to support this movement and oppose those whose "old age" constrained them
to the repetition of slogans that were merely excuses for
inactivity.

"The Left," said Francis Jeanson, "has turned the alibi
of public opinion into a myth. It pretends that public
opinion is not ready. . . . It must not be scandalized. But
the role of the Left was never and is not now to be a slave
of opinion. Its role is to tell the public the truth, however
bitter. It must arouse and support the people." [8]

Jeanson and his friends were all the more convinced of this since it seemed that a segment of public opinion was beginning to change. The reaction set off by the discovery of the network was considerable. The press, on both the Right and the Left, discussed it at length, and letters to the editor were not all unfavorable to the network. The U.N.E.F. came out strongly against the war. Also propaganda encouraging insubordination was increasing, especially in the Latin Quarter. Some students had been arrested for participating in the seditious movement known as Jeune Resistance.

Books about this kind of refusal were published: *Le Refus, Le Déserteur, Le Passager de la nuit.*[9] Then in September there appeared the declaration on the right of insubordination in the Algerian war, called the "manifesto of the 121." "We respect and think justified the refusal to bear arms against the Algerians," it stated, because "the cause of the Algerian people, which has contributed in a decisive way to the breakdown of the colonial system, is the cause of all free men." Among the first signatures were those of Jean-Paul Sartre, Simone de Beauvoir and almost all of the editors of *Les Temps Modernes.* On September 5 the trial of the "Jeanson network" began, and from then on, the trial and the declaration were one in the mind of the public.

While the press was giving generous coverage to the trial, there appeared the first declarations of those who signed the "manifesto of the 121." On September 8 *Paris-Presse* entitled one of them: "Jean-Paul Sartre, Simone de Beauvoir and a hundred others risk five years in prison." There was a great scandal. The role of detonator that the partisans of Francis Jeanson had envisaged for themselves seemed to be coming about. First, a number of their theses were brought suddenly before the public. Second, by a chain of interdependent events, a course of action became clear. *L'Humanité* demanded the liberation of the accused who "in their own way fought for freedom"; the young Socialists (S.F.I.O.) "did not approve insubordination but respected it." When government employees who had signed the "manifesto of the 121" were dismissed, the S.F.I.O. and the Communist Party were unanimous in their protest.

Finally, the Left was shaken. Not wishing to be accused of inactivity, it too protested against the war and sided, from a safe distance, with the signers. Another manifesto on the part of students, teachers and trade unionists "for a negotiated peace in Algeria" was signed by such figures as Maurice Merleau-Ponty and Colette Audry. This was intended to be a gesture of solidarity with the "121" though on a broader basis than the declaration on the right to insubordination.

On October 27, as the result of the initiative of the U.N.E.F. and different non-Communist organizations of the Left, 15,000 people gathered in and around the Mutualité in Paris to protest the continuation of the war. The Communist Party and the C.G.T. also organized local demonstrations.

During this period, the editors of *Les Temps Modernes* might have thought that their work was going to prove effective, that something was going to change. Marcel Péju wrote that, "In this autumn of Gaullism . . . the balance of opposing forces gives the momentary impression that everything is possible." [10] And Sartre declared: "It is important to say as clearly as possible that these men and women [those accused in the Jeanson trial] are not alone, that hundreds of others are continuing their efforts and thousands are ready to do so. An adverse fate has temporarily separated them from us but I dare say that they are our delegates in the defendants' box. What they represent is the future of France. The ephemeral power that is pretending to judge them no longer represents anything." [11]

But the fever soon subsided. The campaign for the insubordination on the part of those who had been called to serve in the war in the autumn of 1960 was a failure. The press no longer spoke of the network. The demonstration of October 18 remained without issue.

But the French existentialists continued to fight. In the summer of 1960 Sartre and Simone de Beauvoir had gone to Brazil to speak for those in France who were opposed to the Algerian war. They spoke about anticolonialism and met with representatives of the G.P.R.A. This was an answer to the propaganda tour Malraux had made in Brazil a short time before. Sartre continued these good-will trips; in the autumn of 1960 he went to Italy and spoke on the same platform as Boulharouf, the representative of the F.L.N.

Simone de Beauvoir continued her work on the Committee for Djamila Boupacha, a young Algerian woman who had been tortured.[12] *Les Temps Modernes* was still very much preoccupied with the Algerian question; it reworked in depth positions it had previously taken and continued to criticize the "respectable Left." They carried on in spite of the small public reaction, and despite the fact that the Communist Party considered their positions contrary to the spirit of unity. The fundamental stance of *Les Temps Modernes* was "the position which could not be

abandoned because it was demanded by rational analysis—
it was a question of the mind and not of the heart—was
solidarity between the Algerian and French peoples." [13]

This solidarity was all the more insisted on because
Les Temps Modernes, itself socialist, thought that the
campaign waged by the F.L.N. should lead logically to a
socialist transformation. That is why the journal undertook to explain the F.L.N. and espoused its cause on every
important issue. That is why it violently denounced the
role of the *harkis*, reacted vigorously against the repression
of Algerian demonstrations on October 17, 1961, and published communiqués by the French Federation of the
F.L.N. This is also why Claude Lanzmann approved and
saw value in the hunger strikes of Algerian prisoners.

After the Algerian demonstrations on October 17, 1961,
Sartre, in cooperation with Laurent Schwartz and the
Comité Maurice Audin, organized a silent demonstration
of protest for November 1. With Simone de Beauvoir he
participated in the great mass demonstrations at the end of
1961 and the beginning of 1962—on November 18, in the
demonstration organized by the young Communists and
Socialists (P.S.U.); on December 19 in that organized by
some unions and supported by the Communist Party and
the P.S.U.; and finally in the enormous march on February 13 which protested the assassination by the police of
nine anti-fascist demonstrators.

By their actions the *Temps Modernes* existentialists
invited a good deal of vehement hatred. Sartre's apartment
was bombed by the O.A.S. and threats increased. For some
time now the demonstrators of the extreme Right had
ended their rallies with the shout: "Shoot Jean-Paul Sartre!"
If the Right and Center[14] were indignant about the existen-

tialists, so was the "respectable Left." To *L'Express*, which defended a more moderate line and urged the Algerians to surrender, *Les Temps Modernes* replied that unlike *L'Express*, they had no advice to give to the G.P.R.A. The S.F.I.O. had privately circulated brochures peevishly comparing Jeanson to the collaborators, and the F.L.N., the enemy of France, to the Nazis.

But along with their denunciations and their daily combat, the French existentialists were trying to reflect upon the situation and to discern its implications for the future. They asked themselves serious questions about all aspects of the Algerian revolution, and about the economic change and general direction they should seek. "For," as Jeanson wrote, "our aim is evidently to reach a real definition . . . which will enable us to place the problem of Algerian development *in a perspective of action*." [15] This perspective was to be "resolutely socialist and opposed to neocolonialism."

Then came the cease-fire in Algeria. The French, Sartre wrote, had been "unable to hasten the cease-fire; the whole history of our times has passed them by and they stumble like sleepwalkers toward their destiny. . . . It must be understood that we have today the only chance of regenerating ourselves: We must control the army's loyalty by uniting *to guarantee the execution* of the agreements signed. On this condition the cease-fire will also be the start of the beginning for us." [16]

There would be no real beginning if "the Algerians won their freedom [and] the French lost theirs." Furthermore, had the Algerians won all their freedoms? Was Ben Bella's a government of a social democratic Republic? Marcel Péju thought so: "I would not change a word in my analysis of the Algerian revolution." He was convinced that the revolution was beginning and that "Évian [was] Brest-Litovsk." Péju gave his full support to the political program of Ben Bella and collaborated on the weekly *Révolution Africaine,* which had its headquarters in Algiers.[17]

Jean-Paul Sartre dissented from this position: "We do not think that the present situation in Algeria favors the development of the revolution. There is an interval. . . . But there are reasons for the halt of the revolution." He gave, as these: the economic state of the country, which encouraged (perhaps even necessitated) authoritarianism; the F.L.N.'s lack of a detailed program; the structure of the recent war; the fact that the only individuals prepared to take power were outsiders who had been organized either in the prisons or in the border armies. Those within had been pulverized by the war. "We neither want to hide these things nor furnish fresh grounds for attack as does Jean Cau," Sartre continued. "This interval in the revolutionary process tempts us to a friendly neutrality. We never intended to take a position in favor of the Party of the socialist revolution because it does not have the masses behind it and is a divisive factor. In any case, it is certain that things will not improve unless the situation becomes more revolutionary." [18]

But action was not easy either for the French people or for *Les Temps Modernes,* because, as Jeanson explained, "we are dealing with the Algerian revolution, which is to say a revolution that can only be brought to a happy conclusion by the Algerian people themselves." The conditions for assistance were very different from those that obtained during the war.

But Sartre and Jeanson saw something that could be done immediately: a demand for amnesty for all who were exiled or imprisoned because of their anticolonialism. Such people could be useful in bringing about cooperation between the French and Algerians; Jeanson commented, "It is impossible to imagine that their sentences can be maintained because this would be neither reasonable, rational nor economical. I know many people who could and were asked to work usefully for Franco-Algerian cooperation; but they hesitated and finally refused because they could not see any sense in going to Algeria and working clandestinely under difficult circumstances. The situation is that our political position has to be taken in secrecy." [19]

On this occasion Sartre once again proclaimed his total solidarity with those who had fought beside the F.L.N. or had refused to bear arms against it. Aware that he had not had mass support during the war, he nonetheless remained convinced of his position: "We do not want to condemn any form of combat, but practically speaking the Left has done nothing. And if we did not have the support of the masses, that was not our fault. . . . I do not think that our effort was greatly efficacious but it nonetheless obliged the Left to take a step forward because of the chain of solidarity that was formed to defend the signatories [of the manifesto] and victims of repression. . . . With respect to the war in Algeria we did what had to be done and that is all." [20]

The editors of *Les Temps Modernes* were profoundly influenced by the Algerian war. One cannot understand Sartre's political attitude without understanding his hatred for the French bourgeoisie. The prolonged silence of the French people and their smug Gaullism were as profoundly repugnant to Sartre, Simone de Beauvoir and their friends as the repression and tortures in Algeria. "The result of the referendum [of September 28, 1958] had severed the last threads linking me to my country," Simone de Beauvoir wrote in *The Force of Circumstance* and asked herself: "Would I be permitted, one day, to love this country again?" Even people in restaurants manifested their hostility to the two writers and their political positions. They were perfectly at one with one another in the midst of a blind nation. Only the million Parisians who filled the streets on February 13, 1962, proved that perhaps all had not been in vain. "My God!" wrote Simone de Beauvoir in recalling this demonstration, "How I had hated the French! I was overwhelmed by this suddenly recovered sense of brotherhood."

Notes

1 · Jeanson, F., *Algérie hors la loi* (Paris, Seuil, 1955).

2 · See Sartre's letter to the military tribunal during the trial of the Jeanson network in *Le Monde*, September 22, 1960. See also an interview he gave to *Vérité Pour*, a clandestine monthly edited by Francis Jeanson, No. 9, July, 1959. Among other things, Sartre said: "I find it incredible that Leftists are disturbed by the nationalism of the Algerians. To be sure this nationalism, like all historical realities, includes contradictory elements. But what should be important for us is that the F.L.N. conceives of an independent Algeria in the form of a social democracy . . . . if Algerian nationalism bothers certain Leftists, who should recognize in it their own experience and past, it is by no means because we have become pure universalists. Rather, and here we must rid ourselves of all mystification, the real reason is *our* nationalism."

3 · Jeanson, F., "Lettre à Jean-Paul Sartre," *Les Temps Modernes*, Nos. 169–170, April–May, 1960, p. 1537.

4 · Sartre, J.-P., in his preface to *Aden Arabie*, by Paul Nizan (Paris, Maspero, 1960), p. 56.

5 · Sartre, J.-P., in his preface to *Damnées de la terre* by Frantz Fanon (Paris, Maspero, 1961), p. 22.

6 · Jeanson, F., "Lettre à J.-J. Servan-Schreiber," *Vérité Pour*, No. 17, July 26, 1960.

7 · Some examples: "Réponse à Jean Daniel," an article signed "Temps Modernes," *Les Temps Modernes*, Nos. 169–170, April–May, 1960, pp. 1530–34. In "Une Gauche respectueuse" (of the same issue) Marcel Péju took to task *L'Express*, Maurice Duverger, Gilles Martinet, Étienne Fajon and several others. The June 13, 1960, issue of *Vérité Pour* contained "Lettre à une camarade" (an answer to Madeleine Riffaut of *L'Humanité*), an article entitled "Réponse à quelques objections," a letter by Robert Davezies to Hubert Beuve-Méry, and a letter by Francis Jeanson to J.-M. Domenach in reply to Domenach's article in *Esprit*. The July 26 issue of *Vérité Pour* contained two letters by Francis Jeanson in reply to *France-Observateur* and *L'Express*.

8 · Arnaud, G., "Les Étranges Confidences du 'Professeur' Jeanson," *Paris-Presse*, April 20, 1960, a report on a clandestine press conference by Francis Jeanson.

9 · Maurienne, L., *Le Déserteur* (Paris, Minuit, 1960); Maschino, M., *Le Refus* (Paris, Maspero, 1960); Pons, M., *Le Passager de la nuit* (Paris, Julliard, 1960). *Les Temps Modernes* reviewed these books. See Givet, J., "Trois livres d'une actualité glaçante," *Les Temps Modernes*, No. 171, June, 1960, pp. 1855–58. Several months later Claude Faux, then secretary to Sartre, published *Le Réseau*, a book on the problem of aid for the F.L.N. (Paris, Julliard, 1960).

10 · Péju, M., *Le Procès du réseau Jeanson* (Paris, Maspero, 1961), p. 12.

11 · Sartre, J.-P., "Lettre au tribunal militaire," *op. cit.*

12 · The committee was launched with an article by Simone de Beauvoir, "Pour Djamila Boupacha," published in the "Libres Opinions" section of *Le Monde* on June 2, 1960. The book *Djamila Boupacha* (Paris, Gallimard, 1962) documented the case and published reports on the committee's activities. It was co-authored by Simone de Beauvoir and G. Halimi.

13 · Naury, J.-P., "Entretien avec Jean-Paul Sartre," *Tribune Étudiante*, an organ of the students of the P.S.U., Nos. 5–6, January–February, 1962.

14 · In this respect we might cite a significant article by Pierre Hervé on Sartre in *Le Nouveau Candide*, December 29, 1961. Entitled "What Makes Sartre Delirious?" the article accused him of being the F.L.N.'s "best lawyer." "It is no longer a question of politics; Sartre is hallucinated." The article dragged in psychoanalysis to prove that Sartre's antics were "the expression of infantile conflicts." Further, Sartre was a demagogue who thrived on scandals. Hervé used the occasion to mull over the abortions, child murders and homosexual acts described in Sartre's novels. Why all this? Because Sartre "has a father complex, and his father is de Gaulle."

15 · Jeanson, F., *La Révolution Algérienne*, "Problemes et perspectives" (Milan, Feltrinelli, 1962), p. 15.

16 · Sartre, J.-P., "Les Somnambules," *Les Temps Modernes*, No. 8, April, 1962, p. 1401.

17 · Péju had quarreled with Sartre in June, 1962, over personal matters but also over the positions he had taken, as secretary general of *Les Temps Modernes*, on the clandestine anticolonial movements and his choice of Ben Bella. The June, 1962, issue announced that he was being dropped from the editorial

committee of the journal and being replaced by Francis Jeanson.

18 · During an interview in February, 1963. Francis Jeanson analyzed the situation in a similar fashion. But he noted that the economic condition of Algeria was such that even French capitalism was interested in preventing economic, social and political chaos there and that cooperation was a strict necessity. Jeanson continued to insist that the reconciliation of the two wings of the F.L.N. was the only way of letting the people speak and vindicating the revolutionary character of the party.

19 · During a press conference held at the home of François Tanguy-Prigent, a former minister; it was held on January 21, 1963, with the participation of various public figures, including Sartre, insubordinates and deserters. This conference attracted a good deal of attention and the whole Leftist press reported it and published articles on the problems it raised.

20 · During an interview in February, 1963.

Chapter

10

THE BROKEN MIRROR
OF THE LEFT

DURING THE LAST PERIOD of the Algerian war, in spite of
the polemics and arguments among the different currents
on the Left, the *Temps Modernes* group was convinced
that it had to cement alliances and encourage the enthusiasm and unity of all who opposed the Gaullist regime and
colonialism. They proved their resolve by initiating moves
toward those who did not share in their precise political
positions. Sartre participated in the National Congress for
Peace in Algeria through Negotiation, which was held on
June 11 and 12 at the Mutualité. Organized by the Comité
Pleyel, this meeting was a preparation for an antiwar demonstration to be held on June 28, 1960. The committee, to
which Sartre had always belonged, had taken similar initiatives in 1958 and 1959. In 1960 it was reinforced by men
of such varying persuasions as Raymond Guyot, Claude
Bourdet, Jules Isaac, Jacques Kayser and André Philip.
Consent for the demonstration had been given by the
C.G.T., the Communist Party, the P.S.U., the S.F.I.O. and

the unions of the C.F.T.C., among others. Sartre had also been a member of the executive committee of *Verité-Liberté* from its beginning, along with a certain number of non-Communist intellectuals.[1]

These were negative signs of unity. Sartre was simultaneously attempting a political *rapprochement* with the Communist Party. These efforts were made easier by the fact that the situation in Hungary was improving while the politics of repression in Algeria and the danger of fascism were getting worse. His initiative was slow and at first not too clear. It seems to have begun in 1958. In July, 1959, Sartre was willing to say that Russia, despite all its contradictions, could be considered a socialist country, and the Communist Party, on its side, actively sought dialogue. In André Gisselbrecht's words: "We regret that other progressive intellectuals do not enlist their services like Sartre. We must work for the triumph of Marxism together." [2]

On the level of daily politics, anti-Gaullism served the cause of *rapprochement*. *Les Temps Modernes* called for a negative vote on the referendums of January 8, 1961, and October 28, 1962. Finally, the necessity of fighting against fascism and the awareness that it would be harmful to cut themselves off from the masses helped bring about improved relations with the French Communist Party.

All of this led *Les Temps Modernes* to participate in a mass organization with the Communists and the non-Communist Left (with the exception of those influenced by the S.F.I.O.). In fact on December 4, 1961, as a result of efforts on the part of intellectuals within the Communist Party, 250 university students and intellectuals founded the Ligue d'Action Pour Le Rassemblement Antifasciste. It included, in addition to the representatives from *Les Temps Modernes* and the Communist Party, various figures from the extreme and moderate Left and members of the P.S.U. The League's aim was to facilitate the united action of the French Left against fascism.

On February 11, 1962, the League called an assizes for the purpose of organizing the multiple anti-fascist committee that had sprung up just about everywhere into a federation under its aegis. As it turned out, the representatives of the Communist Party, fearing that the influence of Leftist intellectuals like Sartre would predominate, succeeded in having, in addition to the League, the Front Universitaire Antifasciste Étudiant (F.U.A.), the French organizations of the Comité Anticolonialiste, and other committees and groups call an assizes for the constitution of a new assembly.

The assizes of February 11, 1962, was called upon to determine democratically: ways of coordinating the action and organization in the battle against the O.A.S.; the manner in which university students and intellectuals could contribute to the unity of the democratic forces and promote a renewed democracy; and a course of action to bring about peace in Algeria.

But the latent conflict between *Les Temps Modernes* and the Communists soon broke out. The former wanted the organization to be relatively centralized (to give it more weight), proclaim itself resolutely hostile to the government, and emphasize solidarity between the French and the Algerians. The Communists would have none of this. They pushed for an assembly with a broad basis and a reduced program. *Les Temps Modernes* also hoped that the organization would not be limited to intellectuals but include committees from the working class. This was the most serious point of disagreement, especially since some of the representatives of the P.S.U. supported the Communists. No doubt the latter were afraid that if the doors were open to the working class the C.G.T. would be heavily in the majority.

It is clear that *Les Temps Modernes* had not abandoned their "disrespect" toward the different parties. Their explicit intention was to oppose any limitation to the fight, "to envisage the elements of radical action," and to seek out contacts with the C.G.T. in order to convince certain of its members.

The divergences were in part overcome by compromise, but it was clear that the movement was to be a university movement, intellectuals and students fighting side by side with the working classes and the principal democratic organizations. It took as its name the Front d'Action et de Coordination des Universitaires et Intellectuals pour un Rassemblement Antifasciste (F.A.C.U.I.R.A. or, more simply, F.A.C.). "They tried to imprison us in a ghetto of intellectuals," was Sartre's comment at the time.

The F.A.C. elected a directing committee of seventy members which, one week later, elected a subcommittee of twenty-eight members including Sartre (his deputy was Claude Lanzmann) and Jean Pouillon.

The divergences continued and crystallized around the problem of solidarity with the Algerians and the role of the organization (should its decisions be unanimous, as the Communists wished, or determined by the majority, as recommended by *Les Temps Modernes*, the P.S.U. and others?). The F.A.C. was not very effective. Its problems paralyzed it and were never resolved. The subcommittees of the F.A.C. discontinued their meetings after July, 1962. Sartre considered the whole project useless.[3]

But it is important to note that Sartre readily cooperated with the Communists within this organization while at the same time reserving his right to criticize them, always with the intention of forcing them to toughen their line of action. Certainly *Les Temps Modernes* still maintained that the Party had not renewed its methods, that it was still afflicted with sclerosis. But the editors also made it clear that they wanted to cooperate as closely as possible with the French Communist Party. They could not become members—nor, for that matter, would the Party have wanted them—but Sartre remained convinced that "if we do not work with them, we will revert to a false Left that leads nowhere. If we do not work with the Party we will slip to the Right." [4] For the Party was still the only absolute enemy of the capitalist regime and the only one that resolutely retained a conception of class. "What I deeply respect in every Communist," Sartre said, "is that he risked everything by joining the Party and deliberately made himself the whipping boy of all bourgeois societies." [5]

But since the French Communist Party remained contemptuous and Roger Garaudy, a member of its central committee, was convinced that Sartre had lost faith in the future of the working class, *Les Temps Modernes* sought closer ties with Communists outside of France. They found them first of all in Poland. Then they gradually established close political rapport with the Italian Communist Party, whose leaders had, since the Liberation, shown a kind of friendship to *Les Temps Modernes* that was never extended by the French. "If I were in Italy, I would join the Party," Sartre told me.

The journal gave a good deal of space to analyses of the Italian Party. For example, an article by its secretary general, Palmiro Togliatti, appeared in the February, 1962, issue. In the double issue of September–October, 1962, on "Data and Problems of the Working-Class Struggle," five of the eleven authors were Italian.

Sartre and Simone de Beauvoir often traveled to Italy and took part in discussions on culture by the Italian far Left (Communist or not). Sartre published numerous articles in the Italian Communist papers on such topics as the assassination of Julian Grimau and the Russian film *My Name Is Ivan*. When in March, 1964, the Italian Communist press issued a collection of political articles by Sartre (including his condemnation of the Soviet intervention in Hungary), *L'Unità*, the official organ of the Italian Communist Party, interviewed Sartre (can one imagine *L'Humanité* doing that?) and gave the book a favorable critique. Sartre was invited by the Instituto Gramsci (the Italian Center for Marxist Studies and Research) to speak about the problems of Marxism and his views on morality and society. Russian, Polish and Czech as well as Italian Communists participated in the discussion.

Sartre eulogized Palmiro Togliatti in *L'Unità* the day after his death. He had had great admiration for Togliatti, and considered the Italian Communist Party the only alive and effective Communist Party in Western Europe. One has only to compare the tone of this article with a telegram Sartre sent the French Communist Party after the death of Thorez to see the profound difference in his feelings.

It was through the Italians that Sartre renewed contact with the Soviet Communists. In June and July of 1962 he spent nearly a month in the Soviet Union as the guest of the Soviet Union of Writers. "Was this your first trip to Russia?" *Libération* asked him when he returned.

"No. The second. The first was in 1954."

"Have you noticed any changes since your last visit?"

"Indeed I have. In 1954 the welcome was very warm but somewhat formal. . . . This time, by contrast, I noticed that the conversation was freer, more comprehensive and open. It was more adventurous than predictable."

"Did you get the feeling that there has been a thaw?"

"Exactly. The ice has been broken between us." [6]

In his Moscow speech to the World Congress for General Disarmament and Peace Sartre tried to contribute to the thaw and to peaceful coexistence by defining conditions of cultural competition that would in the end benefit Marxism. The first thing to do would be to stop subverting culture to the ends of the cold war. Kafka had been used as a military instrument against Soviet Russia. Sartre urged that culture be "demilitarized," that exchanges take place, that instead of rejecting Kafka altogether Marxism judge him more objectively and profit by his work. For "if the cold war has not resulted in many deaths . . . it has congealed universal culture." Culture must become human once again.

This speech was considered important in the Eastern countries. It opened a path for dialogue, not only between French and Soviet writers, but between socialist intellectuals in general. The speech was published in East Germany and Stefan Hermlin, a member of the Literary Academy and the translator of Éluard, drew a whole new theory of social realism from it. Social realism, he concluded, is everything that pertains to human culture, everything that is antireactionary; this was an attempt to transcend the kind of naturalism in which social realism is too often lost.

Kurt Hager, a member of the Central Committee of the Unified Party of the R.D.A., attacked this as a too liberal, indeed "bourgeois" interpretation. But Hermlin refused to change his position.

And in the Soviet Union, despite the severe "warnings" given to literary innovators, a colloquium on the novel was held at Leningrad in August, 1963, at which Sartre, Simone de Beauvoir and Alain Robbe-Grillet were present. Once again the threads of a dialogue were taken up. Sartre opposed bourgeois literature and at the same time attacked the old-guard Soviet writers. He defined what he thought should be genuine socialist literature, and cited as a proto-type of such literature Soljenytsine in Matriona's *La Maison*.

A translation of Kafka appeared in the Soviet Union. Sartre and Simone de Beauvoir were received by Khrush-chev. The thaw continued and dialogue was well on its way.

"When the cold war began," Simone de Beauvoir wrote when she returned from this visit, "we backed the U.S.S.R. Since it began to change over to a peace policy and become de-Stalinized, our doubts about this choice had ceased; its cause and its opportunities are ours too; our stay this time turned this bond into a living friendship. A truth is rich insofar as it has *become*; it would be wrong to think of the conquests of the Russian intellectuals as small: those con-quests include all the obstacles they have vanquished. . . . In Russia man is in the process of making himself, and even if he is encountering difficulties on the way, even if there are hard knocks to be taken, relapses, mistakes, all the things surrounding him, all the things that happen, are heavy with meaning." [7]

And Sartre added: "History is tragic. Hegel said this.

So did Marx, who added that it always progresses with its worst foot forward." But Russia remains "the only great country where progress means anything." [8]

In December, 1963, Sartre and Simone de Beauvoir gave a series of lectures in Czechoslovakia and were warmly received. Sartre even spoke on the national radio and Michel Bosquet reported that the day after one of his lectures students told a professor: "Finally someone has been able to interest us in Marxism." In June, 1964, Sartre and Simone de Beauvoir returned to the Soviet Union. But this distinct improvement in Sartre's rapport with Russia was nothing compared to his feelings for the Cuban revolution. Sartre and Simone de Beauvoir visited Cuba for more than a month in February, 1960, as guests of the journal *Revolución,* and proclaimed their total agreement with the regime. "The revolution is not only a success but an example," she said.

Sartre had numerous discussions with Fidel Castro. He saw and studied the problems of the country and decided to speak widely about them in an attempt to reach as large an audience as possible. He published an article in *France-Soir* to explain the revolution at the time of Cuba's first serious crisis with the United States. Sartre defended Cuba with zest: "I do not see how any people today could pursue a more urgent objective nor one more worthy of its efforts. The Cubans must win or we lose everything, even hope." [9] Sartre returned to Cuba the next year and took a strong stand against the invasion of the island in April, 1961; and even when Castro adopted Marxist-Leninism he saw no reason to change his opinion on the Cuban revolution.

Sartre's attitude toward some of the socialist countries

was clear: He approved of revolutions wherever they took place and wherever they were alive. He approved the Communist Parties to the extent that they were de-Stalinized. The socialist regimes, "by interiorizing the terror that weighed upon them," paid dearly for this incarnation. It was the price of that "long and decisive terror." But insofar as they remained socialist regimes, it was not possible to be neutral toward them. Every effort had to be made to de-Stalinize them. As Cuba and Algeria proved, Sartre also attached great importance to the problems of the "third world" and decolonization. This was all an integral part of a general political position that the existentialists had developed over a period of years.

This position was resolutely Marxist since that alone took into account the capital fact that men make their own history on the basis of antecedent circumstances. The philosophy of Sartre and the existentialists was formulated within the framework of historical materialism, and the whole *Critique de la raison dialectique* was intended to show "that a negation of negation can be an affirmation, that conflicts within an individual or a group are the motor force of history, that each moment in a series must be *understood* in terms of its initial moment and is irreducible to that moment, that history operates at each moment from totalization to totalization." [10] The *Critique* endeavored to lay the dialectical foundations for a structural anthropology as the basis of dialectical reason. Thus existentialist thought "merged with Marxism and wanted to become part of it" all the while fighting against "the most routine kind of analytic mechanism" which poisoned Marxist thinking in France. The existentialists were not interested in "revising" Marxism but in *creating* it, for Marx and Engels had be-

queathed an infinite task to intellectuals of their own age as
well as others.

The "orthodox" intellectuals of the French Communist
Party did not think that these infinite tasks were be-
queathed to Jean-Paul Sartre in quite the same way as to
themselves. They insisted that the existentialists remain
existentialist and refrain from meddling with historical
materialism, since their interference was awkward. The
Communists denounced "the aberrant Sartrian attempt to
base historical materialism in an *a priori* fashion on a kind
of transcendental sociology which is the exact opposite."
Lucien Sève found in all of this an "extreme presumptious-
ness," that it was moreover "a little brief, in fact more
than brief: it was nil," that in any event many things were
"outrageous." [11] *La Critique de la raison dialectique* was
called "the talisman of the unhappy consciousness [which]
pretended to be a complement to Marxism but in fact
abandoned it altogether," for Sartre "returns to pre-Marxist
forms of speculation and turns dialectic on its head." [12] On
the other hand, during a congress of Marxist intellectuals
in 1962 Garaudy told Sartre that "there is nothing closed,
completed or definitive in the laws of dialectic. The laws
we know presently constitute a provisionary balance sheet
of our knowledge. Only social practice and scientific
experiment will enable us to enrich them. The most positive
result of meetings like this one is to create the conditions
by which we can contribute to this enrichment together."
How was it that Marxism could be enriched by a partner
whose philosophy implied "a total abandonment of it"? It
seemed a difficult task.

In fact, the orthodox intellectuals and the leaders of
the French Communist Party wanted it both ways. Sartre

was called a "termite" in 1956 by Marcel Servin, then secretary of the organization. In February, 1957, Maurice Thorez accused him of falling into "old Trotskyite divagations." But in 1960 Roger Garaudy wrote that he did not want to forget the essential tie because of these criticisms: "However profound our differences," he said, "what ought to unite us is stronger than what divides us." Then in 1963 Léo Figuières lumped Sartre with "the modern revisionists whom the bourgeoisie accept with open arms." The French Communists basically reproached the existentialists of *Les Temps Modernes* for not, "even though they were sincere, even passionate enemies of the scandal of capitalism . . . [having] joined forces with the working class and its Communist avant-garde who alone are capable of liberating man." [13]

The existentialists of *Les Temps Modernes* were only slightly impressed by this kind of criticism. Sartre and Simone de Beauvoir participated in a debate on literature organized by *Clarté*, the organ of the Union of Communist Students, at a time when the Party was trying, and not without success, to liquidate one student wing whose antidogmatism displeased it. *Les Temps Modernes* continued to publish its analyses on subjects that others tried to avoid and to recall certain principles and objectives. In March, 1963, they remarked that they did not pretend that "in vigorously reaffirming [these principles] the Left would suddenly spring forth with new life but [they were sure that] it would collapse otherwise." Now that the war in Algeria was over (and the energy expended in fighting it could be directed to other channels), it was necessary to study the problems of capitalism that the war dissimulated "under the more visible structure of fascist threats." [14] It is in this perspective that we must understand the many studies published by *Les Temps Modernes* on the problems of the peasants and the December, 1961, issue on "The Problems of Capitalism" as well as subsequent articles on the trade unions, students and university reform.

Finally too the editors of *Les Temps Modernes* made an effort to clarify the role of the working class in industrialized countries. Criticizing traditional approaches to this matter, they tried to integrate and use the newer ideas of the C.G.I.L. (the Central Socio-Communist Union of Italy) and devoted two remarkable double numbers to "Data and Problems of the Worker's Struggle" and "The Problems of the Worker Movement." They also ran André Gorz's articles on the workers and neocapitalism.

The most important problem was the strategy the workers should adopt toward the expansion of the monopolies. The worker movement could no longer count on the growing misery of the people to provoke social revolution. Even so, the workers' alienation was as great as ever, power was still concentrated in the hands of an exploiting class, and the working masses were still deprived of the means of leading the quality of life that would be possible if the potential of the economy and of civilization was realized. Against the anarchic power of the monopolies, against the law of profit which irrationally regulates the importance and purpose of investments, André Gorz affirmed that the only possible recompense for the working class was a compensation of power. Monetary compensation only consolidated the system. But this goal could not be achieved in one fell swoop by an armed and insurrectionist revolution. To hold forth this type of revolution as a possibility—as the C.G.T. and the Communist Party in France did—amounted to adopting an abstract and abstentionist attitude toward global politics. This in turn could only lead to opportunism and a dispersion of energies in primitive skirmishes without any real perspective.

The working classes cannot share in the management of the economy unless structural reform provides a feasible foundation for the power of the workers against the power of the employers. In fighting for these reforms they should not compromise with a system of mixed economy but should work for deeper change and exacerbate the class struggle. These structural reforms "will not make up a strategy nor escape being pulled back into capitalism unless they are at the outset understood as successive steps toward a socialist society that gives them a meaning and which must be concrete and clear at each step"; in the light of this meaning each intermediary objective is transcended with a view to the next conquests; "otherwise all past conquests will be useless." [15] These conquests will not succeed unless the working class effectively confronts "the transformations brought about by technological upheavals" and takes the initiative "by announcing its availability as leaders." [16] Socialism is the constant perspective of all struggles and must be defined concretely. The French existentialists, with their Italian comrades, were of the opinion that no valid socialist model for the industrialist countries had ever existed. "Politically, socialism is the power of the working class; economically, it is the collective ownership of the means of production, which is to say the end of exploitation. But it is more than that—it is also a new kind of relation between men, a new order of priorities, a new model of life and culture. If it is not

all of this, it loses its meaning." Society ought to be the
end of and not a mere means to production. "Socialism until
now has been no more than a gigantic effort of public
accumulation" and "an infrastructure that often functioned
badly." It has now become urgent "to transcend this
warlike socialism that only thrives on scarcity. . . . The
perspective and compensations of the worker movement
can and *must* be better than existing socialist societies in
their ability to construct socialism." [17]

Nevertheless, since "the passage to socialism cannot
take place immediately nor by armed insurrection, but
only over a long period of time, and that marked by bitter
struggles, the so-called politics of peaceful coexistence . . .
is the only one that is acceptable to us." [18] Peaceful coexistence restores to each worker movement its full and
total sovereignty and makes it responsible for socialism
in its country, a socialism which can never be imported
from the outside. To reject peaceful coexistence would
be to accept war, that is to say, the possible end of humanity, or small wars which have never achieved anything,
as the case of Korea proved so well. The official doctrine
of the Soviet Party puts a brake on revolutions in the
"third world" and postpones them.[19] There is no clear
solution in sight for the capital problem of hunger in the
world. And the Chinese argument, which is based on that
fact, "however specious and aberrant it sometimes is, makes
us aware of our guilt and of real historical contradiction."
Socialist revolutions in the "third world" are not possible
and the principal drama must therefore be played out in
the industrialized states. We must "ask two-thirds of the
world to be patient." We are "morally and ideologically
wrong but politically right." [20] Thus for the working class

in the West there is only one possible policy: to fight for peace, encourage peaceful coexistence which will thaw the worker movements, criticize the contradictions of capitalism and transcend these contradictions in view of a superior society.

The battle ahead would be a difficult one. Neocapitalism suffered only one serious defeat—in the Italian elections of April, 1964. The West is characterized by a strengthening of the powers of the monopolies, by the proletariat's more or less successful effort to integrate and "by that particular form of managerial authority" which Sartre called the *organization*. The revolutionary parties are marking time, repeating clichés and succeeding only in dissimulating with pseudo-revolutionary terminology a reform that lacks purposiveness (this is especially true of the French Communist Party). The direct consequence of the bourgeois offensive and the lack of political worker representation is obvious. The mental and intellectual level of Europeans declines because of a lack of interest in politics, and the *organization*. The a-political atmosphere forces us to accept a state of affairs that no humanist society could accept. The country is in the grip of tortures, and it is well known that three self-confessed executioners have just been acquitted. To be sure, there were protests, but they are always the same and accomplish nothing. Four years ago we could say: The people do not know. But today the people do know and still nothing is changed. Formerly they had the benefit of the doubt. But by informing them of the facts we reduced them to a level of inferior dignity. For they have now accepted the facts. "The present level is the minimum of a humanist culture. We have now reached a critical state." It did not seem that at this level things had changed appreciably since the end of the Algerian war. No awakening had taken place.

In French political life this resignation and cowardly disinterest was symbolized by Gaullism, which greatly profited by it. Only an organized force with a policy of true renewal could put an end to it. *Les Temps Modernes* was chiefly concerned with preventing the Left "from denying itself on the pretext of satisfying current whims."

For *Les Temps Modernes* the legislative elections of 1962 marked the reorganization of the Right. Gaullism was merely the end product of the evolution of the Fourth Republic. It would therefore be pointless to try to patch up the old regime even though one tried to renew it in the process. The former leaders of the parties, today anti-Gaullists, were suspect at *Les Temps Modernes*: "M.R.P. radicals or Mollet-type socialists—they are all former or future supporters." Nothing could be done without a unified and regenerated Left, and in 1962 unity did not seem possible. In the January, 1963, issue, an editorial concluded that, "It was not only relative and circumstantial but came from the outside rather than within; the always broken mirror of the Left merely reflected the real unification of the Right."

The regeneration of the Left made little headway during the elections. The international situation—the aggravation of the Sino-Soviet conflict and the breakup of the socialist bloc, Khrushchev's departure and the immobility of Soviet policy, the impotence of the Soviet Union as well as China with respect to American intervention in Vietnam and Santo Domingo—was of no help whatsoever. The revolutionary reflux was appreciable in Africa and the politics of the "third world" taken as a bloc was floundering. Before all of this, the American government took great pleasure in rediscovering methods that one thought had been abandoned.

In the divided socialist countries, de-Stalinization was making no progress and they were politically stagnated. But the problems that Stalinism had concealed for a period of twelve years were becoming more and more visible. The need for solutions was urgent, both for the socialist countries themselves and for the strategy, theory and practice of the international worker movement.

France was mired in Gaullism. The Left oscillated between various forms of "realism." Some, like Gaston Defferre, wanted to liquidate everything—except a few pernicious habits—under the pretext of adapting. Guy Mollet, like Defferre, was tempted strongly toward a middle line. François Mitterand wanted to come to a hasty compromise that promised little for the future, would make the Communists the counterbalance and furnish everyone the opportunity to brandish yesterday's symbols. There would be little opportunity to confront the problems of a modern industrial society. On both sides the question of a truly unified offensive on the Left was avoided or swept aside.[21] The Communist Party made no effort to shake off its lethargy or understand the situation. Like the Soviet Party, it remained incapable of analyzing Stalinism within its own structures and abandoned the making of the modern society to those who used it for their own purposes and opposed the Party.

Les Temps Modernes saw serious problems in this situation. To be sure, priority should be given to fighting political apathy and false objectivity. But positions on the other questions were more difficult to formulate. The

French existentialists were well aware that they risked confusing politics and ethics. They floundered in the situation and had not yet thought out a strategy that could have helped them at that point.

The evolution of industrial countries in the West, the inadequacies of socialism after the Twentieth Congress and the importance of the "third world"—taken together, these posed an entirely new problem which the Left confronted in impotence. Discussion would have to be taken up where it had been cut off or dissimulated by Stalinism, and without hiding the fact that much precious time had been lost. Many things needed to be rethought. Society had to be understood and seen for itself, else it would be foolhardy to elaborate a political program and strategy. "We must," Sartre said, "rediscover a kind of seriousness in commitment, without losing a certain violence. But it will no longer be romantic, as was the violence of the Resistance or the Algerian war. Much as this may be regretted, it is no longer appropriate for *our* situation, although it still is for, say, the Vietnamese. We must find a rational violence." [22]

Thus *Les Temps Modernes* considered it their immediate duty to contribute to research and to cry out to keep the Left from remaining ignorant, divided and stagnant and thereby signing its own death warrant. They were to serve the Left, but also to forewarn it.

Notes

1 · *Vérité-Liberté,* a journal for information on the Algerian war, began publication in May, 1960.

2 · Gisselbrecht, A., "Les Séquestré d'Altona," *La Nouvelle Critique,* a review for Marxist militants, No. 111, December, 1959.

3 · This seems to be a somewhat harsh judgment. While nothing political was accomplished, there were certain material results: Several million old francs and more than three tons of medical supplies were shipped between March and May to war victims in Algeria. This is appreciable if we bear in mind that Russia sent only six tons of medical supplies during the same period.

4 · "Entretien avec Jean-Paul Sartre," *La Voix Communiste, op. cit.*

5 · Sartre, J.-P., "Grimau," in the Italian Communist journal *Rinascita,* reprinted in *Libération,* April 27–28, 1963.

6 · Interview with Sartre by Paul Morelle, *Libération,* July 11, 1962.

7 · Beauvoir, Simone de, *Force of Circumstance,* tr. Richard Howard (New York, Putnam's Sons, 1964), pp. 638–39.

8 · Sartre, J.-P., "Discussion sur la critique à propos de *L'Enfance d'Ivan,*" *L'Unità,* October 9, 1963. A translation of this article appeared in *Lettres Françaises,* December 26, 1963, and January 1, 1964.

9 · Sartre, J.-P., "Ouragan sur le sucre," *France-Soir,* June 28–July 15, 1960.

10 · Sartre, J.-P., *Critique de la raison dialectique* (Paris, Gallimard, 1960), p. 115.

11 · Sève, L., *La Philosophie Française contemporaine et sa genèse de 1789 à nos jours* (Paris, Sociales, 1962), p. 248.

12 · Garaudy, R., *Questions à Jean-Paul Sartre précédées d'une lettre ouverte* (Paris, Clarté, 1960), Nos. 30 ff., p. III.

13 · Sève, J., *La Philosophie Française contemporaine, op. cit.,* p. 252.

14 · Naury, J.-P., "Entretien avec Jean-Paul Sartre," *L'Express,* March 15, 1962. Merleau-Ponty saw things similarly. He spoke

of the necessity of "becoming aware of the new situation in French society" and of the effort needed "to confront these fundamental problems, which the Algerian war both expresses and masks and which will remain intact after the war is over." See Merleau-Ponty, M., "L'Avenir du socialisme," *Les Cahiers de la République,* XXII, November–December, 1959, p. 32.

15 · Gorz, A., *Stratégie ouvrière et néo-capitalisme* (Paris, Seuil, 1964), p. 93.

16 · Gorz, A., in his preface to Nos. 196–197 of *Les Temps Modernes,* September–October, 1962, p. 402.

17 · Gorz, A., *Stratégie ouvrière et néo-capitalisme, op. cit.,* pp. 17, 22–23.

18 · Gorz, A., in his introduction to No. 204 of *Les Temps Modernes,* a special issue on the Sino-Soviet debate, May, 1963, p. 1923.

19 · The French existentialists attached great importance to the "third world." Their attitude during the Algerian war was an example of this. Nor did their interest cease after the war. Sartre wrote long prefaces to Lumumba's speeches ("Lumumba et le néo-colonialisme" and "Discours de Lumumba") reprinted in *Situations V* (Paris, Gallimard, 1964), pp. 194–253.

20 · Gorz, A., in *Les Temps Modernes, op. cit.* André Gorz added that "we are wrong to be right and the Chinese are perfectly right to be wrong" (p. 1939). The existentialists were fond of describing this sort of ambiguity between the world and politics. Thus Sartre wrote in 1950: "The Communists are guilty because they are wrong in their means of being right." ("The Artist and His Conscience," *Situations V, op. cit.,* p. 207.

21 · *Les Temps Modernes* strongly protested against the opportunism and absence of any clear perspective in the Mitterrand operation. See "Un Compromis inutile," editorial signed "Temps Modernes," *Les Temps Modernes,* November, 1965, pp. 769–75. René Andrieu, in *L'Humanité* (November 11, 1965), saw in this position "the distressing spectacle of confusion, impotence and irresponsibility.

22 · During an interview in 1965

Conclusion

EACH CLASS and each group creates its intellectuals "organically," as Gramsci remarked. Each has an elite capable of organizing the rest of society, defining the group's interests and world vision. This intellectual stratum is extremely broad. In a bourgeois Republic, business leaders and those in the liberal professions—naturally over-represented in Parliament—and, in another capacity, professors and teachers, have played out this role.

The ideal is to be found in medieval society. Hierarchichal, synthetic and juridically ordered, medieval society created the ecclesiastic class to be its intellectual representative. An ideology was manufactured, the Bible interpreted and morality determined at the highest levels. The lower clergy proselytized the teachings and all believed they were serving God—usually to the greater profit of the landed aristocracy. The dominant class really and truly dominated, not only economically and politically but ideologically as well. A univocal and totalitarian world view informed a whole society. The Church had a monopoly on culture and education, and she made every effort to subsume these to the ends of an ideology. What was not special to the class, what remained outside as another good of the whole society (i.e., civilization), was constantly annexed, or at least this was the aim. The clergy alone were authorized to teach, and they controlled art and tried to dominate the sciences. Opponents who tried, however awkwardly, to reestablish the distinction between learning and ideology were burned at the stake. All the intellectual activity of the society was confided to men who were designated, ordained, tonsured and marked by the seal of God.

In this day things are more complex and more camouflaged. French society has come through years of class struggle, and the bourgeoisie no longer has the monopoly on culture. Through its parties and trade unions, the working class has been able to form its own autonomous intellectual leadership. This element informs the class's consciousness and builds it up as an independent force.

Marx had said: "The ideas of the ruling class are in every epoch the ruling ideas: i.e., the class, which is the ruling material force of society, is at the same time its ruling intellectual force." But the working class stands over and against the dominant class as a counterforce. Each class forms its own intellectuals, the only difference being that the bourgeoisie have universities available to them to do the job. However, intellectual camps get into bitter intramural disputes. Intellectuals, whole classes of them, pass bag and baggage from one side to the other and back again.

Until now I have spoken of intellectuals as those who represent the organizing elite of a group, but this is a very broad usage. And at this level it is relevant to take socioeconomic considerations into account. These intellectuals are bound up with social relations, with the form of a society. They give their homogeneity to the class, are identified with it practically, are its *structure*. It is rare for one group to seduce the other's intellectuals, and then done for only very specific reasons. We could scarcely imagine a large segment of the working class selling out to big business; nor, by the same token, could we expect the business or ecclesiastical establishment to put itself at the service of the working class.

But there are other intellectuals who are more or less exempt from social pressures. These are the intellectuals' intellectuals—the "active ideologists." These individuals produce a creative, or at the least an original linguistic formulation of what would otherwise remain confused and unexpressed tension and need. At this level ideologies are literally manufactured, and sometimes truth is arrived at, a truth that is profoundly motivated by the past and the culture of the society but which finds expression and clarity through these intellectuals. Such a truth ceases to be an obscure reflection and strives to become conscious. The image is created, then filtered down through intermediaries to the rest of society. The intellectual as ideologist must be somewhat removed from the new society to which he wishes to give expression, so that he can see it as completely as possible. He seeks a real or supposed universal. He is sensitive to those forces which seem to him capable of incarnating this universal and furnishing him with its material foundations. It is no accident that these intellectuals were all on the side of the Resistance and frequently among its most radical supporters. "When the rising class becomes conscious of itself," Sartre has said, "this self-consciousness acts at a distance upon intellectuals and makes the ideas in their heads disintegrate."[1] But after the initial *élan*, many switch to the other side or stagnate at some half-way position. This is not infrequent.

The French existentialists must be counted among those who remain constant in their belief that in the long run, despite the ebb and flow of history, the proletariat will one day dominate. They work for the one thing they think will eventually bring about their universal truth. This search is their profession and *raison d'être*.[2]

The history of these last years is muddy. Stalinism threw the international worker movement into confusion. There were difficult and sometimes bloody revolutions. Through all this the worker parties, whether in a state of transition or wedded to outmoded structures, were reluctant to look at themselves as they really were. A truly perfect society or party would have no need of intellectuals since it would be perfectly translucent. If, contrary to the evidence, society or the party simply declares this to be the case, it hastens to banish its intellectuals either by discrediting them or by some kind of violence which might be verbal if not actually physical.

In such a case those who wish to be the critical conscience of the worker movement cannot exercise their role from within, as they should be able. They must do it from the outside and they thus make themselves anathema. This runs great dangers. Jeanson points out that one cannot criticize negatively and not run the risk of being imprisoned by the negative. The intellectuals felt obliged to speak out each time silence became scandalous, and since politicians do not always assume their responsibilities, there are numerous periods of such silence. Then everyone's role is made difficult. The masses are silent; political machines take their place, and the intellectuals, responsible for everything because of these defaults, try to express what the others should be saying. If the force they exert is abstract, it is because all too often they find themselves alone when the situation calls for the participation of all. Hence their weakness, for it is not in their power to bear all these heavy responsibilities. But they at least succeed in protesting and giving warning. Their language was preferable to just staying confused and opting out, even though it committed the same kind of excesses it deplored in others. The intellectuals do sometimes seem to depart from their proper role, but that is only to fill the vacancy, and it is their duty to do so. Merleau-Ponty took cognizance of this when he expressed his opposition to the use of force in Algeria in May, 1958, and proposed immediate political objectives: "But, after all, many people know this much better than I do. . . . Who am I to speak at such length about it? The officers prophesize, the professors sharpen their pens. Where are the counselors of the people, and have they nothing they can offer us but their regrets?" [3]

This function of the true critic is total. He cannot be content to merely denounce the most blatant scandals. He must contend with society as a whole and be held accountable as Sartre remarked in a 1964 interview, for no less than "raising questions in the most radical and intransigent manner." He must create the culture of our times. The existentialists believe that Marxism is a self-sufficient culture, or that it should be, and that in any case it is indispensable. Other systems are outdated, but Marxism has not yet come into its own.

The role of the intellectual is therefore to express and analyze what has not yet come about or only imperfectly, first of all at the level of political analyses. Manifestoes issued after political deliberations are not very enlightening —they are by definition calls to action rather than expressions of thought and are overly simplified, overnegotiated, and deliberately weighted.

The intellectual creates, expresses and discovers. He

works through art to elaborate a culture which would, Sartre says, be "the critical mirror of the total man," a culture in which "man can recognize himself . . . and contest what he sees." Without this, society would be blinded. Merleau-Ponty says that culture is what brings "the world's confused talk to an end with a precise word."

It is neither simple account nor mere reflection, "it is an appeal. It transposes the world on which it leans and in which it is rooted in both its realities and its possibilities. The world that is written about is not the same as the one we customarily see. It is both that world and another: that world as dynamic, off its bases, suspended, questioned." [4] "Art presents the world as it would be if it were conquered by human freedom," Sartre has remarked.

This is an explanation of the existentialists' constant protest. One may not assume values since freedom, and therefore the future, must be constantly reintroduced into the proposition. It is even more impossible to accept elementary givens because this would suppose that the world is already created and finished, its meaning stamped on it like a trademark.

If culture is more than political combat and not merely a form of self-congratulation, it exists as a social reality. When one chooses as the French existentialists chose, if one refuses to think or write for the power elite, one faces what Sartre talked about as early as 1947: For whom does one write? And he answered: "But in the heavens above our modern societies, the appearance of those enormous planets, the masses, upsets everything. Transforming artistic activity from a distance, they rob it of its meaning without even touching the artist's tranquil conscience. Because the masses are *also* fighting for man, but blindfolded, since they are in constant danger of going astray, or forgetting who they are, of being seduced by the choice of the myth-maker, and because the artist has no language which permits him to hear them. He is speaking of *their* freedom—since there is only one freedom—but speaking of it in a foreign tongue." [5]

The most fundamental historical contradiction is that the masses cannot think out their own culture, and that those who can must do so from the outside. There is no congruity between the artist and his public, and this contradiction is aggravated because the instruments of culture are still largely in the hands of the ruling class. When Sartre speaks he cannot be sure to whom he speaks; he cannot choose his audience. Often it is the middle class who applaud his plays. *Dirty Hands* was a typical example. The public destroyed this work by changing its meaning and transforming the play into a cold-war device. The Communists assisted them.

The problem was raised starkly when *Words* was published. The right-wing critics applauded the style and said nice things about Sartre's account of his childhood, but they belittled his politics. Were they really not trying simply to "retrieve" Sartre by awarding him the Nobel Prize in spite of his ideology? When he refused it, their praise turned quickly to anger, and many delighted in putting it down to character as a means of evading the political questions involved. Others were more direct: *L'Aurore* accused Sartre of antipatriotism and Gabriel Marcel joined the chorus, referring to Sartre's "cynical scorn for the truth," his "camouflaged intellectual cow-ardice," and the "dishonesty" of this "gravedigger of the West." [6]

Only the Leftist press tried to understand Sartre's attitude, and even the Communists showed some amount of sympathy.

Sartre had not sought a writer's career, after the Liberation, any more than he had sought a career of political activism. The social structure and political situation had prevented more obvious connections. In any case the act of writing has political implications and, as the French intellectuals pointed out, this kind of implication and commitment has got to be conscious and directed at something. The intellectual strips away disguises in order to change, but one does not inevitably change things by this act of unmasking. It is only through tenuous and complex mediations that word becomes action. Neither silence nor absence can be condoned.

"For a long time I treated my pen as a sword," Sartre has written. "Now I realize how helpless we are. It does not matter: I am writing, I shall write books; they are needed: they have a use all the same. Culture saves nothing and nobody; nor does it justify. But it is a product of man: he projects himself through it and recognizes himself in it; this critical mirror alone shows him his image." [7]

Nor does political activity in itself justify. Nevertheless it is essential; it affirms that man is possible.

Notes

1 · Sartre, J.-P., *Search for a Method,* tr. Hazel Barnes (New York, Knopf, 1963), pp. 18–19.

2 · This does not mean that they become partisans of a proletarian culture as opposed to the culture of the bourgeoisie. As Leon Trotsky said in *Literature and Revolution,* the former has never in fact existed. It is primarily a question of taking a political position and thus laying the foundations for a culture that will transcend all classes and become the first truly human culture.

3 · Merleau-Ponty, M., "Tomorrow," in *Signs,* tr. Richard Mc-Cleary (Evanston, Illinois, Northwestern University Press, 1964), p. 350.

4 · Pingaud, B., "L'Année dernière à Leningrad," an introduction to the interventions of different writers at a seminar on the novel held in Russia in August, 1964, and published in *Esprit,* July, 1964, p. 19.

5 · Sartre, J.-P., "The Artist and His Conscience," in *Situations,* tr. Benita Eisler (New York, Braziller, 1965), p. 209. Reprinted with permission. English translation copyright © 1965 by George Braziller, Inc.

6 · Marcel, G., "Prise de position," *Les Nouvelles Littéraires,* October 29, 1964. Marcel was highly indignant with Sartre, as can be seen from the following: "I do not hesitate to say, after having weighed my words carefully, that Sartre is an inveterate denigrator and a systematic blasphemer. He has spread about him the most pernicious teaching and given the most poisonous advice ever proffered to young people by a patent corruptor."

7 · Sartre, J.-P., *The Words,* tr. Irene Clephane (London, Hamish Hamilton, 1964), p. 172.

Postscript

IN THE YEARS after the Liberation, Sartre's work wavered between the poles of ontology and politics; analyzing freedom and *taking positions* about society; service to literature and service to revolutionary action. A morality that could link these, and make good (or clear) political attitudes was not forthcoming. Even so, and paradoxically, Sartre's influence was largely ethical. *Being and Nothingness* and the articles in *Les Temps Modernes*—and more so the false impression the press gave of Sartre's opinions and work—led a certain segment of youth to deduce from him a moral viewpoint. Sartre was the Bob Dylan of his age. He himself did not sing, but singers who identified with him were listened to. A moral attitude was fashioned that bore the stamp "Existentialism": revolt of adults against society, protest of children against their parents. For many Sartrianism mixed surrealism, absurdity, André Gide and Hervé Bazin.

With the cold war and Korea, Sartre changed. He became a fellow traveler of the Communist Party. His position became official—it was a priesthood, with rites, rules of fidelity and permissions. During the height of Stalinism and McCarthyism it seemed that this kind of position had to be taken. The danger of war was great and the United States was the aggressor; the French government was subject to American power, as was part of the Left and almost all of social democracy.

The Communists were not accepting allies who were

not fellow travelers; they considered it dishonorable that one should place oneself above the fray. Political action in 1950 could not be a trip to Switzerland as it was during the war of 1914. It was easy to cast one's lot with the wrong side. American propaganda flooded public opinion and thrived on threats from the Left. Stalinism had its own internal logic; it demanded to be either totally accepted or totally rejected. The time demanded exclusive loves.

Sartre became a fellow traveler and placed his fame at the service of the Party as Barbusse had done before him. He had no real political influence, but by holding out for the maximum of freedom permitted by the situation, he reinforced the Party's influence and Russia's as well and thus encouraged the cause of peace. This represented neither a quest nor a seminal position; it was a warning and an example; solidarity in a time of crisis. It was precisely the opposite of Flaubert's solidarity with the *bourgeoisie* during the repression of the Paris Commune.[1] Sartre accepted much in order to save something.

After the Hungarian revolt and the Algerian war he no longer thought this attitude possible. When he was truly isolated, he said what he thought, and very few followed him. But aside from the insults hurled at him, it was recognized that he had a right to speak out. If Sartre could not create a political situation, he succeeded in shaking up smug consciences and giving a warning and expression to the revolutionary desires of many young people.

I began to read Sartre in philosophy class. In our society, information always lags behind reality and the manuals are dated. The Sartre I knew—as he could only be known in a provincial city in 1958–59—was the Sartre of the Liberation. The image I had of him, transformed by society, was rather more individualist than political. I took *The Wall* and *Nausea* for Gide, and *Being and Nothingness* for Kant. Roquentin and Erostratus seemed like heroes. As for *Dirty Hands*, the break between Hugo and his father interested me much more than Sartre's relationship with the Party. I approved of Orestes for leaving his people at the end of *The Flies* and going away, alone and useless. Camus' *The Rebel* was for me the logical consequence of *Existentialism and Humanism*. I was convinced for several months that Sartre was still part of a triumvirate that included Merleau-Ponty and Camus. Only afterward did I discover his break with Camus, quite by chance while reading an old issue of *Études*, the Jesuit periodical. I was surprised to hear of Sartre's differences with Merleau-Ponty, and I read them as contemporary events. I later came to know Sartre's political opinions. I became a victim of Sartrolatry. I was at once Sartrist, Sartrien, Sartrologue and Sartrizing. A writer who justified revolt against family, and absolved God's assassin, certainly deserved some credit. I accepted his political positions in blind faith since there were no alternatives. But I was agreeing with the Sartre of 1952 and *Les Communistes et la paix*. I went through a period of Stalinism and believed in it. Sartre did not spare me that, although he helped me avoid its worst aberrations. He had summed up fifteen years of French political life, with the Henri Martin affair, the Hungarian revolt, the 13th of May and the Algerian war. I covered those fifteen years in one or two years.

Our generation still knew Sartre through his first books—*The Wall, Nausea*—and in our preconceived ideas thought of him as a philosopher of the absurd. Later we were to discover his political thinking and his commitment.

He was the only author to interest young people at the early stages of their thinking and rebellion, and to give them some general conception of man and society—the only one to give our rebellion a future by transcending it.

But now things have changed. The generation that is just becoming aware of the problems of our time have a modified image of Sartre; his work is viewed in a more synthetic light. The last years of the Algerian war, *The Condemned of Altona*, the *Critique de la raison dialectique* and *The Words* have changed our first impressions of the Sartrian ideology. Given what we know about Sartre, it is no longer possible to incarnate the Sartrian ideal in the protagonists of *The Wall* and *Nausea* or to be satisfied with a mutilated interpretation of these works. Sartre's subsequent political positions have influenced our understanding of his earlier work and changed its meaning for us. Symbol and sometimes motor force of revolt, partisan of socialism and a radical Left, adversary of the bourgeois system of economy and morality, Sartre has analyzed, thought out and expressed revolt, the Left and hatred of the dominant class. This has become part of his work and gives it political meaning.

Sartre's writings and fictional characters therefore represent a privileged transition for a certain segment of youth, mostly students, to politics. Many students have embraced communism for Sartrian reasons, a communism that is not necessarily "frozen" as the history of the past few years has proven. Sartre once said that the point of departure for many young people today was his own terminus.

To understand Sartre's political role we might contrast it with the kind of political influence exercised by Aragon;

one is the inverse of the other. Aragon, it seems, might have achieved a stature similar to Sartre's: he went from surrealism to communism, from pure revolt to revolution. But, except in a few poems, Aragon was never able to reconcile his literary work with his political positions or, in other words, to relate his fictional characters to the real problems of our age.

Sartre's novels, plays and essays (their classicism and formal structure notwithstanding) confront the human questions of our age. In these works politics is neither thesis nor appendix. It is a dimension of the Sartrian universe precisely because it is a dimension of the world in which we live. Torture, war and social violence are presented in the background in order to gain perspective. Franz in *The Condemned of Altona* is not a timeless hero. Sartre's protagonists are situated in our age. This presence is crucial. Politically this is much more important than membership in a party, even the Communist Party. Sartre renders an account of our history; he unmasks and criticizes it. This is the opposite of the "great intellectual" who may sometimes intervene when scandal or injustice moves him, or of the "humanist of the good French tradition" into which the new criticism would assimilate him. A witness but also partisan, Sartre speaks of a world where man struggles, and where he experiences victory and defeat. This world is of permanent interest.

Sartre's literary writing and his political opinions are part of a total work—partly achieved, partly in the making —that is beginning to be recognized both as a totality and an evolution. The desire for a de-Stalinized communism, the Algerian war, the Cuban revolution, *The Condemned of Altona*, the *Critique de la raison dialectique, The Words,*

Les Troyennes, reflection upon himself and others—in all of this history is made articulate. In literature, as in politics, this is a new phenomenon. Sartre defines a system of renewal, of interpretation and fresh criticism. He implies no deception. Literature does not conceal a political product that must be swallowed to boot. No political pill is hidden in the literary sugar nor does political intervention wear the cloak of literature in order to make itself acceptable. Inseparably both make appeal to the freedom of man.

Note

1 · Sartre had been fascinated by Flaubert for several years. Could it have been out of jealousy? Flaubert detested the *bourgeoisie*, heaped scorn upon them, drew numerous unflattering portraits of them, satirized the stupidity of their organizations and officials and insisted that he was alienated from his class. But in spite of everything he remained a bourgeois, tied to his class by an almost "natural" bond. When his class was threatened, Flaubert rose to its defense without second thoughts.

After 1952 Sartre desired to be similarly tied to the working class. He wanted his destiny to be irrevocably bound up with that of the workers so that no matter what he did or said there could be no escape. Was not his hope to be able to criticize the class, its organizations and representatives, without calling into question his fundamental solidarity with it, without the class being able to reject him even when it disagreed, to be bound to it and at the same time feel himself a stranger to it?

But Sartre did not claim the right to detest, scorn and denigrate the working class as Flaubert did the *bourgeoisie*. Both Sartre's social origin and the political climate of our times prevented him from achieving the kind of integration granted Flaubert, almost in spite of himself. Sartre was cut off from the proletariat. His only link with it was a political party which claimed to be a spokesman for the class, and which in any case would never authorize the kind of freedom Sartre wanted.

Appendix

Sartre and Camus— The Anatomy of a Quarrel

BY BERNARD MURCHLAND

CAMUS AND SARTRE met one another for the first time during a dress rehearsal of the latter's play, *The Flies*, in 1943. This encounter marked the beginning of a famous friendship that was to end notoriously, one might almost say pathetically, less than ten years later. Their relationship was never easy, as Sartre would write at the end. As early as 1945 serious political and ideological differences were apparent between them, and these became more sharply defined as the years went by. In Simone de Beauvoir's words: "If this friendship exploded so violently, it was because for a long time not much of it remained."[1] Nonetheless, it had been in important ways a close and productive relationship. After Camus' death Sartre minimized their quarrel; it wasn't really important, he said, "just another way of living together without losing sight of one another in the narrow little world that is allotted us."[2] Sartre also acknowledged Camus' importance: One had to avoid him or fight him—he was indispensable to that tension which makes intellectual life what it is." [3] In perspective it can be seen that both were in the vanguard of those who took it upon themselves to provide the postwar era with its ideology. The immediate occasion of their final split was the publication of Camus' *The Rebel* in November, 1951. It was highly acclaimed by the critics and Camus apparently expected it would be favorably reviewed by *Les Temps Modernes* as well. When it was not, he wrote a sharp letter to Sartre, the journal's editor, and the friendship was over.

Francis Jeanson, who had agreed to review the book for *Les Temps Modernes,* began his article in the June, 1952, issue with some ironical remarks to the effect that Camus couldn't possibly be as great as the critics claimed, and said that he was highly suspicious of the almost universal praise bestowed upon *The Rebel.* Camus' style, in the first place, was too formal and "transcendental." It was stripped and reduced and bore a merely abstract relationship to reality. Anyone proposing to write about the bloody events of our times in this manner, Jeanson argued, was obviously on the wrong track. There was some fundamental flaw in his vision of things.

The same "transcendentalism," Jeanson went on, was present in *The Plague.* Whereas *The Stranger* had been the story of an "involved subjectivity," *The Plague* was an account of events "seen from on high, by an abstract subjectivity which did not live those events but merely contemplated them." [4] Here, as in *The Rebel*, the style belied a philosophy. By adopting the objective tone of a chronicler, of one who is not in the thick of things, Camus posed as an Olympian observer. Seen from this lofty vantage point, the struggles of men could only seem vain, absurd. To be understood and allievated, such struggles must be lived by the engaged consciousness. Thus, concludes Jeanson, Camus was in a contradictory position both by reason of his style and his conception of existence:

> A Mediterranean spirit, infatuated with intellectual transparence, faithful to solar constancy and the pure light of noonday—but confronted in the real world with contradictions and human suffering—Camus rationalizes the scandal of his reason by representing humanity as unjustly subjugated to the forces of anti-Reason, condemned to Absurdity and Evil in violation of a right which should be his own. This metaphysical evil can only be countered with a "metaphysical honor" which consists in "maintaining the absurd in the world" at the price of a revolt which is also absurd.[5]

Dr. Rieux, the chronicler of *The Plague*, was symbolic of this predicament: he defied the epidemic by trying to save as many lives as possible but he was defeated before he began. His victories, the result of a temporary and capricious permission from the gods, would in the end be swept away. In such a fatalistic universe there was at bottom nothing to be done and all experiences were equivalent. Man was condemned *ab initio*.

The same contradiction characterized *The Rebel*. The basic flaw in Camus' argument, Jeanson proceeded to show, was its *antihistoricism*. History was viewed in such a way that it was suppressed as such; concrete situations were ignored in favor of a pure, Hegelian play of ideas deprived of their dialectical vigor; the sufferings of men dissolved in an abstract metaphysics. Camus evidently did not believe in infrastructures, Jeanson pointed out, and ignored the historical and economic causes of revolutions (which was another way of saying that Camus didn't understand Marx). His methodology was such that he continually confused theory and practice and in the end ignored the essence of all revolution: namely, "the circumstances that give rise to them, their concrete development and the human element that makes them effective."

Jeanson expressed the opinion that Camus' flirtation with history during the Resistance left a bad taste in his mouth which he attempted to wash away with the highly speculative formulae of *The Rebel*. His *tour de force* was to have translated historical revolt into metaphysical rebellion and thereby caught himself up in an irreducible dilemma. The basis of Camus' position, Jeanson noted, was his "passive antitheism." He did not deny God since such a being was necessary to establish one pole of Camus' equation of absurdity; nor did he accept Him since that would have made his stance as a "revolted slave" meaningless. Thus, "if God is the absolute executioner who, in condemning man to death and inflicting the torture of Absurdity upon him, from the beginning and forever subjects him to absolute injustice, it becomes difficult to take the relative injustices of the world seriously and rather vain to try to remedy them." Jeanson went on to show himself infuriated by what he took to be Camus' static, eternalistic view of history in which "the revolutionary is both the victim and the dupe of God because he strives to equal Him in power and cannot succeed in doing so. The rebel, on the other hand, is the victim who rises up in an attitude of permanent defiance which does not give God the satisfaction of contemplating His failures since in this case nothing is attempted and consequently there can be no failure." [6] History thus became, for Camus, a species of the Absurd which must be faced with Sisyphian resistance since all evil was to be found in history and all good outside of it.

For Jeanson this was tantamount to a rejection of history as such. Consequently he felt called upon to urge Camus "to become a historically situated conscience." History is the work of man, he explained. It is man "who gives it a relative consistency by transcending each historical event in terms of its total meaning, an act that implies postulating a certain future and unmasking a certain past and a certain present." Man makes history and history makes man, or more accurately "remakes" him. On Jeanson's interpretation, Camus would have us avoid such recreation by venturing nothing. The attitude of the rebel might have a positive, disciplinary value provided it "enters into the context of history and there determines its objectives and chooses its adversaries." Otherwise, it wears itself out in a vain effort to become transcendent.

In his letter to the editor of *Les Temps Modernes*, Camus retorted with some justice that the thesis of his book had been distorted. In an icy remark that set the tone of his response, he said that the only way his book could be considered "an antihistorical manual and a catechism for abstentionists" was if it had been rewritten in that sense by the reviewer. He rejected the charges laid against *The Plague* ("If there is an evolution from *The Stranger* to *The Plague* it is in the direction of solidarity and participation") and protested that Jeanson "had energetically refused to discuss the central theses" of his book—the definition of limit, his criticism of post-Hegelian nihilism and Marxist prophecy, the analysis of dialectical contradictions and his critique of the notion of objective culpability. He recalled that his book was intended to be a study of "the ideological aspect of revolutions" rather than an empirical description of the revolutionary phenomenon itself and cited evidence that ideologies also have an important role in the formation of social consciousness. Camus wondered why Jeanson reviewed the book since he ignored what he read in it and insisted on calling black what Camus himself had called blue. He was further puzzled by the fact that his critic took the central thesis of the book to be a proposition (all evil is in history and all good outside of it) which much of the book is concerned with refuting. "*The Rebel*, in fact, proposed—and more than one hundred quotations would prove this if necessary—to demonstrate that pure antihistoricism, at least in the world today, is as bad as pure historicism. . . . Anyone who has read my book seriously knows that for me nihilism coincides with disincarnate and formal values." Camus explained further that his book did not deny history (that would be meaningless) but criticized those who would make history an absolute.

Camus accused *Les Temps Modernes* of "defending Marxism as an implicit dogma without being able to affirm it as an open political policy." To support the first part of this accusation he pointed to the reviewer's (he never referred to Jeanson by name) inclination to classify all critics of Marxism as Rightists, his insistence that idealism is a reactionary philosophy and his failure to discuss any revolutionary tradition other than Marxism. As proof of the second part of his accusation, Camus noted first that the review refused to seriously discuss Marxist and Hegelian theses and take a position on them. He asked: "Is there or is there not such a thing as Marxist prophecy and is it not contradicted today by many facts? Does *The Phenomenology of Mind,* or does it not, authorize a theory of political cynicism and were there or were there not Left-Hegelians who influenced twentieth-century communism?" An important distinction in *The Rebel* between Marx's critical method, which was an important contribution, and his utopian messianism, which was dubious in the extreme, was not discussed by Jeanson. Why? Are Marxist dogmas so sacrosanct? Whoever takes Marxism seriously must criticize it, especially Marxists, and this, Camus asserted with some vigor, the reviewer resolutely avoided doing.

A further, and indeed more serious, argument in support of the second part of Camus' accusation was Jeanson's failure to discuss the phenomenon of suffering and the specifically political implications of authoritarian socialism. Camus recalled that his book was a detailed study of the relationship between revolution in the twentieth century and terror and suggested that no one, whether he was for or against the book, had the right to ignore this important issue. Camus had in mind principally the Soviet work camps but also the fact that revolution today presupposes terrorism and ends by enslaving millions of men. He put his case in sharp syllogistic form: "You reserve the relative right to ignore the concentration camps in Russia so long as you do not raise the problems posed by revolutionary ideology in general, and Marxism in particular. You lose this right if you raise such questions and you raise them in talking about my book."

The polemic, it has now become clear, turns on the question of revolutionary ideology. This, in turn, involves a philosophy of history. In an important passage, Camus comes to the heart of the matter:

To legitimate the position he takes toward my book, your reviewer should demonstrate . . . that history has a necessary meaning and a final outcome, that the frightful and disordered face of contemporary history is merely apparent, and that, on the contrary, it inevitably progresses, although with ups and downs, toward that moment of reconciliation that will mark the advent of ultimate freedom. . . . Only prophetic Marxism (or the philosophy of eternity) could justify the pure and simple rejection of my position. But could this be clearly and without contradiction affirmed in your journal? For after all, if man has no end that can be taken as normative, how can history have a presently definable meaning? Or, if it has one, why shouldn't man make it his end? And if he did so, how could he remain in that state of terrible and unceasing freedom you speak of?

Camus insisted that these objections were of capital importance. The point is this: Does history have an end or not? He recalled his argument in *The Rebel* that the sacrifices demanded in the past and today by revolutionary Marxism could only be justified in view of an eventual happy ending of history while the Hegelian and Marxist dialectic excluded such an end. Camus opined that the reason why Jeanson failed to discuss this point was that his professed existentialism could not accommodate any historical purposiveness. To reconcile Marxism with existentialism he was forced to defend this difficult thesis: History has no end, but it nonetheless has a meaning which is not transcendent to it. Camus admitted that such a position might be defended; but so long as it was not the review of his book remained vitiated by a contradiction which favored nihilism. "To free man from all shackles only to imprison him practically in historical necessity is equivalent to first of all depriving him of his reasons for fighting only to deliver him to the mercy of any party whose only rule of operation is efficacy. This is in conformity with the law of nihilism according to which one goes from extreme freedom to extreme necessity. And this is nothing other than the resolve to manufacture slaves." And Camus continued:

> The truth is that your reviewer would have us revolt against everything but the Communist Party and the Communist State. He is as a matter of fact in favor of revolt as indeed he must be considering the condition [of absolute freedom] prescribed by his philosophy. But he is tempted by the kind of revolt which takes the most despotic historical form; and how could it be otherwise, since for the time being his philosophy gives neither form nor name to this fierce independence? To revolt he must do so in the name of the very nature which existentialism denies. Hence he must revolt, theoretically, in the name of history, but since no one can revolt in the name of an abstraction, universal significance must be predicated of history. Then history becomes the sole rule of action and is thus deified; in his revolt man must abdicate before those who claim to be the priests and Church of such a God. At the same time, existential freedom and adventure is denied. As long as you have not clarified or rejected this contradiction, defined your conception of history, accepted or excluded Marxism, do we not have every right to say that, no matter what you do, you remain imprisoned by nihilism? [7]

Camus pressed on to his conclusion with heated prose. He was tired, he said, of all this double talk, of seeing seasoned militants (who had given all to the struggles of their age) lectured and censored by armchair theoreticians. He made it clear that he was pleading on behalf of those for whom history was a cross rather than a thesis subject. All men, he said, are in search of truth. Our common task ought to be the defense of whatever slim chance there might be for success in this enterprise. This at any rate was the point of his book and assuredly the point of his letter to *Monsieur le Directeur*, Jean-Paul Sartre. "We will certainly not combat the insolent masters of our time by distinguishing between their slaves," Camus concluded. "This would be tantamount to distinguishing between the masters themselves and thus resigning oneself to a preference that should be openly admitted as such."

It was a closely reasoned and strongly worded argument. Sartre was obviously stung. In the same issue of *Les Temps Modernes* he published his now celebrated "Reply to Albert Camus." [8] If for no other reason, it deserves notoriety for some of the most acrid *ad hominem* argumentation in twentieth-century writing. On the first page we read: "Your combination of dreary conceit and vulnerability always discouraged people from telling you unvarnished truths. The result is that you have become the victim of a dismal self-importance, which hides your inner problems, and which you, I think, would call Mediterranean moderation." Sartre, presumably fortified by the traditional Gallic intuition into truth, proceeds to demonstrate to Camus the error of his ways: "A formal and violent dictatorship has established itself in you, dependent upon an abstract bureaucracy, and which claims to bring about the reign of moral law." Sartre envisaged Camus as a doctor pointing out the corpse's (i.e. Jeanson's) wounds to an astonished audience. And he goes on: "It is totally immaterial to you, is it not, that the incriminated article does or does not discuss your book? The latter is not on trial. A god has vouchsafed its value. Your book will serve only as a touchstone to reveal the bad faith of the guilty party." And again: "Tell me, Camus, for what mysterious reasons may your works not be discussed without taking away humanity's reasons for living? By what miracle are the objections made to you transformed within the hour, into sacrilege?"

Sartre questioned Camus' right to criticize the Communist Party or to speak on behalf of the suffering masses. He also objected to the fact that Camus had not directly answered Jeanson. "You call me Monsieur le Directeur, when everyone knows we have been friends for ten years. I agree, it is only a device. You speak to me when your apparent subject is to refute Jeanson. That is a dirty device. Is it not your real aim to transform your critic into an *object*, a dead man? You speak *of him* as though he were a soup tureen or a mandolin, but never *to him*." And then the outburst: "But I ask you, Camus, just *who* are you to stand off at such a distance? And what gives you the right to assume, apropos of Jeanson, a superiority which nobody accords you? . . . Are you so afraid of being challenged? Must you hastily devalue all those who look straight at you and only accept those who look at you with bowed heads?" Sartre ends the first movement of his rejoinder with a defense of his position on the Soviet camps and the suggestion that Camus might find happiness in the Galapagos islands.

Phase two opens with a defense of Sartre's concept of human liberty. Camus' confusion on this question, he writes, stems from his "mania for not going to the source." Sartre suggested that his book, *Being and Nothingness,* contains an adequate account of this problem. But "reading it would seem needlessly arduous to you; you detest difficulties of thought, and hastily decree that there is nothing in them to understand, in order to avoid the reproach in advance of not having understood them." Sartre then goes on to maintain that "our liberty today is nothing except the free choice to fight in order to become free" and "we must accept many things if we hope to change a few of them." Camus, on the other hand, had argued that while freedom is a legitimate goal it cannot be guaranteed "by accepting many things" for this is precisely the error of ideological radicalism and ends by accepting totalitarianism as the historical instrument of liberty.

The differences between the two men are made clearer by a long section of Sartre's reply in which he recalls Camus' biography. During the war years, much united them. Camus was then an "admirable conjunction of a person, an action, and a work." To a war-torn and weary Europe this Camus proclaimed the duty of happiness, the necessity of fighting injustice and the fraudulence of abstractions. Through the Resistance he entered into history and by the same token into solid union with all who bore the welts of historical injustice. "How we loved you then," Sartre writes. "We, too, were neophytes of History and we endured it with repugnance. . . ." But gradually, Sartre continues, Camus began to identify the forces of absurdity with an abstract and intolerable destiny. He protested against heaven when he should have blamed men. At this juncture antihistoricism began to paralyze his message. In this way "what had a short time before

been an *exemplary reality*, became the totally empty affirmation of an *ideal*. . . . You decided against History,
and rather than interpret its course, you preferred to see
it as one more absurdity." Consequently, "only half of you
lives among us, and you are tempted to withdraw from us
altogether, to retreat into some solitude where you can
again find the drama which should have been that of man,
and which is not even your own any more." And: "You
view History with distrust, you dabble a toe which you
pull out very quickly and you ask, 'Has it a meaning?'
. . . And I suppose that if I believed, with you, that History is a pool of filth and blood, I would do as you do, and
look twice before diving in."

Sartre then clarified his own conception of History,
which is, he believes with Marx, "only the activity of man
pursuing his own ends." History on this view becomes a
matter of living it rather than asking whether or not it has
a meaning, of giving it an objective rather than supposing
that it has some theoretical end. Man "makes himself historical in order to undertake the eternal, and discovers universal values in the concrete action that he undertakes in
view of a specific result." History is something that one is
already in. To assert, in an *a priori* fashion, that its course
is unjust is already to have lost the game, to have accepted
"a world without justice" against a "justice without content." Our duty is "to give History that meaning which
seems best to us, by not refusing our participation, however weak, to any concrete action which may require it."
Because Camus had rejected History, Sartre feels obliged
to pass judgment upon him: "You are no longer anything
but an abstraction of revolt. Your distrust of men makes
you presume that every defendant was, before the fact,

a guilty man. From this stemmed your police tactics with Jeanson. Your morality first changed into moralism. Today it is only literature. Tomorrow perhaps it will be immorality."

Jeanson closed the debate with a lengthy article in which he attempted to clarify his original accusations. But he failed to make any substantial contribution.[9] Thus the polemic ended, for all practical purposes, with Sartre's "Reply." It may fairly be said that Sartre did not answer Camus. In fact he does not seem to have understood him. He argued as though *The Rebel* were a slightly modified version of *The Myth of Sisyphus* (in which case some of his objections would have been valid), whereas it represented a remarkable advance in Camus' ethical thinking. We may well wonder about this misunderstanding. What motivated Sartre to take the simplistic position he did? Personality dispositions undoubtedly had a good deal to do with it. Nicola Chiaromonte suggests that the answer "must be found in the phenomenology of the amateur Communist."[10] By that he means one who is a freewheeling liberal operating within the Communist ideal, one who owes the Party no official allegiance but nonetheless is convinced that it alone promotes the objectives of peace and justice. I think there is some merit in this suggestion. However, I would argue further that the real root of clash resides in the fact that Sartre is amateur ethicist as well. His dispute with Camus was basically a dispute about values.

Simply put, they disagreed over the ethical worth of man. *The Rebel* advances an ethics while Sartre adheres to the conviction that in an absurd universe no ethics is possible. The controlling metaphors of his thought are those of nausea and entrapment. To live is a disgusting business. And there is no way out of it. In *Being and Nothingness* Sartre offers two radically incommensurate modes of being (being-in-itself and being-for-itself) as his basic ontological postulates. This initial distinction (which he has never abandoned) provides the framework of all of his later speculations and precludes a resolution of the ethical problem. For him, the knowing mind collides with the contextual world. The sheer spontaneity of consciousness, that limpid world where anything goes and nothing is justified, gives rise to the experience of anguish in which the isolated self apprehends the horrible and empty reaches of responsibility and gazes enviously upon the solidity of things about it. It is in fact a nightmarish world in which the integrity of a structural world has collapsed. Man is that being whose past is dissolved in the lucid apprehension of the moment which in turn is lost in a hurtling project toward the future, that being whose lack of being renders his choices and values utterly contingent and without connection in the manifold of reality, a creature whose impossible striving toward concidence with being is the basis of his alienated predicament. We expend ourselves in a vain effort to reach completeness and totality and in trying to accomplish this goal we are exposed to all the vultures of constant striving. In Sartre's own words: "The being of human reality is suffering because it emerges in being as perpetually haunted by a totality which it is without being able to be it. . . . Human reality therefore is by nature an unhappy consciousness, without the possibility of surpassing its unhappy state." [11] *

* *Note:* I realize, of course, that Sartre's ethical thinking has appreciably matured since *Being and Nothingness*. His many political

Camus knew all about the absurd world and explored it rather thoroughly. But unlike Sartre, he could not remain content with the ambiguous and forlorn consequences of absurd premises. He rejected the ethics of pure freedom, which was as unpalatable to him in all forms. Sartre continues to maintain that man has no stable nature and possesses no constant tendencies. As Professor Wild puts it: "There are no changeless norms to which he can look for the guidance of his conduct. To set up such norms is merely to rationalize choices that have already been made. Liberty itself is the only stable norm. To maintain this is always good." [12] Camus analyzed this categorical imperative as a last instance in a long history of Western hubris, a species of that voluntaristic extremism that infects those who strive imperiously for divine status. He came to realize that there is no way in which temporal striving can be adequate to absolute demands; no way in which spiritual significance can be satisfactorily abstracted from the natural, specific and unique experience

---

writings since then, and especially the first published volume of his *Critique de la raison dialectique* (1960), are serious efforts to give empirical content to his theory of freedom. By attempting to reconcile the individualistic tenets of existentialism with the social orientation of Marxism, Sartre is effectively elaborating an ethics of action. However, I am not convinced that he has succeeded very well. In other words, his theory of freedom seems to be substantially what it always was: a form of voluntaristic idealism. In any event, it was the "idealist" Sartre of *Being and Nothingness* who quarreled with the "realist" Camus of *The Rebel* in the early 1950's. Whether or not their disagreement would resolve itself today is another question. For two recent assessments of Sartre's ethics see *Principles and Persons,* by Frederick A. Olafson (Baltimore, The Johns Hopkins Press, 1967) and *Reason and Violence: A Decade of Sartre's Philosophy 1950–1960,* by R. D. Laing and D. G. Cooper (London, Tavistock, 1964).—B.M.

of the world. If the long history of Western thought has proven anything, it has proven that that way lie the many variations of damnation, the principal modern manifestation of which Camus took to be legitimate and wholesale murder.

Thus *The Rebel* proposed "to face the reality of the present, which is logical crime, and to examine meticulously the arguments by which it is justified; it is an attempt to understand the times in which we live. One might think that a period which, in a space of fifty years, uproots, enslaves, or kills seventy million human beings should be condemned out of hand. But its culpability must still be understood. . . . It is incumbent upon us to give a definite answer to the question implicit in the blood and strife of this century." [13] The discussion was historically oriented from the outset. Camus established the cause of historical revolution during the past two centuries in a romantic quest for totality which has resulted in despotic and apocalyptic ideologies. In rebelling against the old absolutism (e.g., divine right of kings) the revolutionaries substituted a new absolutism. Starting from the premise of unlimited freedom they arrived (not illogically) at unlimited despotism. It is this unlimited character of revolutions, one might almost say their wantonness, that Camus deplores. And he urges rebellion instead, a rubric that summarizes the principal tenets of his moral position. In a pithy statement he notes that in rebellion the slave rises against his master (because he recognizes a worth in himself that is being denied) but in revolution, the slave aspires to take his master's place (i.e., introduce a new tyranny for the old). It is the principle of all revolutions, Camus argues, that human nature is infinitely malleable or,

what comes to the same thing, that there is no human nature:

> Absolute revolution, in fact, supposes the absolute mal-
> leability of human nature and its possible reduction to
> the condition of a historical force. But rebellion, in
> man, is the refusal to be treated as an object and to be
> reduced to simple historical terms. It is the affirmation
> of a nature common to all men, which eludes the world
> of power . . . Man, by rebelling, imposes in his turn
> a limit to history, and at this limit the promise of a
> value is born. It is the birth of this value that the
> Caesarian revolution implacably combats today be-
> cause it presages its final defeat and the obligation to
> renounce its principles.[14]

Camus postulates a human nature with an accompanying value pattern as an answer to the blood-letting madness of modern history. And in this he harkens back to
the Hellenic emphasis on limit and moderation. "Rebellion,
at the same time that it suggests a nature common to all
men, brings to light the measure and the limit which are the
very principle of this nature." [15] When any claim to absolute freedom is made, the destruction of all value is
heralded. Both Christianity and Marxism, in Camus' view,
"postpone to a point beyond the span of history the cure
of evil and murder, which are nevertheless experienced
within the span of history." [16] Man is a relative creature;
he should have learned by now that to taste of Absolute
fruit is to poison the wells of human creativity and prepare
the path to nihilism. We must relearn that the first condition of being a man is to refuse to be a god. This philosophy of finiteness, the law of due proportion, is the final

theme of Camus' moral theory. It is summarized in the closing lines of *The Rebel*:

> We shall choose Ithaca, the faithful land, frugal and audacious thought, lucid action, and the generosity of the man who understands. In the light, the earth remains our first and our last love. Our brothers are breathing under the same sky as we; justice is a living thing. Now is born that strange joy which helps one live and die, and which we shall never again postpone to a later time . . . With this joy, through long struggle, we shall remake the soul of our time, and a Europe which will exclude nothing.[17]

The issue of history was central to this debate. But this in turn, as Camus pointed out and Sartre denied, necessarily involved an ethics. If Sartre defines history as "only the activity of man pursuing his own ends," then Camus would seem to have good reason to wonder what these ends are. To say again that we give history "that meaning which seems best to us" also raises the question of what that meaning is. In his reply Sartre said: "A brake cannot be applied to liberty. It has no wheels. Neither has it hoofs or jaws in which to put a bit." Camus called this "liberty without restraint" and equated it with nihilistic revolution. Thus it was most fundamentally the Mediterranean Camus who offended Sartre, the Camus who advocated and spelled out a moderate ethic. To make oneself historical "in order to undertake the eternal" was in Camus' eyes another way of playing God and legitimatizing the horrors of absolutist inquisitions.

In retrospect, it can be seen that Sartre was both poorly disposed and poorly equipped to answer Camus. Thus from a tactical point of view, Camus would have been wiser to deal directly with Jeanson. But the issues would have been identical. And in any event the debate was doomed to end on the note of hostility and irresolution. This is unfortunate because it dealt with questions of the utmost importance for our times. Specifically, it dealt with two incompatible views of man. In one sense this debate is as old as philosophy itself (compare, for example, Socrates and Thrasymachus in *The Republic*); in another sense, it is a continuing dispute. Until we have reached some satisfactory agreement, everyone who is concerned with the course of history will be a participant in the quarrel between Sartre and Camus.

Notes

1 · Beauvoir, Simone de, *Force of Circumstance,* tr. Richard Howard (New York, Putnam's Sons, 1964), p. 259.

Miss de Beauvoir goes on to analyze the differences between the two men in these words:

Camus was an idealist, a moralist and an anti-Communist; at one moment forced to yield to History, he attempted as soon as possible to secede from it; sensitive to men's suffering, he imputed it to nature. Sartre had labored since 1940 to repudiate idealism, to wrench himself away from his original individualism, to live in History; his position was close to Marxism and he desired an alliance with the Communists. Camus was fighting for great principles . . . usually, he refused to participate in the particular and detailed political action to which Sartre committed himself. While Sartre believed in the truth of socialism, Camus became a more and more resolute champion of bourgeois values; *The Rebel* was a statement of his solidarity with them. A neutralist position between the two blocs had become finally impossible; Sartre therefore drew nearer to the U.S.S.R.; Camus hated the Russians and although he did not like the United States, he went over, practically speaking, to the American side. . . . These differences of opinion were too radical for the friendship between the two men not to be shaken. (*Ibid.,* p. 260)

We may assume that Miss de Beauvoir's words are a faithful echo of Jean-Paul Sartre's sentiments.

2 · Sartre, J.-P., "Tribute to Albert Camus," in *Camus: A Collection of Critical Essays,* ed. Germaine Brée (New York, Prentice-Hall, 1962), p. 173.

3 · *Ibid.,* p. 174.

4 · Beauvoir, Simone de, *The Prime of Life,* tr. Peter Green (London, Penguin, 1962), p. 562.

5 · Jeanson, Francis, "Albert Camus: ou l'âme revoltée," *Les Temps Modernes,* No. 79, June, 1952, p. 2074.

6 · *Ibid.,* p. 2085.

7 · Camus, Albert, "Lettre au Directeur des *Temps Modernes,*"

Les Temps Modernes, No. 82, August, 1952. The following six remarks quoted of Camus are taken from the same source, pp. 323–33.

8 · Sartre, J.-P., "Reply to Albert Camus," in *Situations,* tr. Benita Eisler (New York, Braziller, 1965), pp. 71–112. All quotations are from that source.

9 · Jeanson, Francis, "Pour tout vous dire," *Les Temps Modernes,* No. 82, August, 1952, pp. 354–83.

10 · Chiaromonte, Nicola, "Sartre versus Camus: A Political Quarrel," in *Camus: Critical Essays, op. cit.,* pp. 35 ff.

11 · Sartre, J.-P., *Being and Nothingness, op. cit.,* p. 550.

12 · Wild, John, "Existentialism as a Philosophy," in *Sartre: A Collection of Critical Essays,* ed. Edith Kern (New York, Prentice-Hall, 1962), pp. 146–47.

13 · Camus, Albert, *The Rebel,* tr. Anthony Bower (New York, Vintage, 1956), pp. 3–4.

14 · *Ibid.,* p. 250.

15 · *Ibid.,* p. 295.

16 · *Ibid.,* p. 303.

17 · *Ibid.,* p. 306.

Index

About the Author

MICHEL-ANTOINE BURNIER, born in 1942, was edu-
cated at the University of Paris and at the Institut d'Etudes
Politique de Paris, and was the editor of *Les Nouveaux
intellectuels,* published in 1966. In addition, he has written
for *Les Temps Modernes, Clarté* and, presently, *L'evene-
ment.*

BERNARD MURCHLAND teaches at Ohio Wesleyan
University. He is the editor of *The Meaning of the Death
of God,* and *Two Views of Man.* He translated *The Drama
of Vatican II* by Henri Fesquet as well as many other books
from the French. He has written for *Commonweal, world-
view* and other journals of opinion.

Date Due